ARCHERY

Steps to Success

W9-DIF-351

Kathleen M. Haywood, PhD
University of Missouri–St. Louis

Catherine F. Lewis, MEd
Andrews Academy
Creve Coeur, Missouri

Leisure Press
Champaign, Illinois

Library of Congress Cataloging-in-Publication Data

Haywood, Kathleen.
  Archery: steps to success/Kathleen Haywood, Catherine Lewis.
    p. cm.—(Steps to success activity series)
  Bibliography: p.
  ISBN 0-88011-324-3
  1. Archery. I. Lewis, Catherine, 1957-   . II. Title.
III. Series.
GV1185.H38 1989
799.3′2—dc19   88-647

Developmental Editor: Judy Patterson Wright, PhD
Production Director: Ernie Noa
Copy Editor: Peter Nelson
Assistant Editor: Kathy Kane
Proofreader: Laurie McGee
Typesetters: Sandra Meier and Yvonne Winsor
Text Design: Keith Blomberg
Text Layout: Denise Mueller
Cover Design: Jack Davis
Cover Photo: Bill Morrow
Illustrations By: Pam Shaver and Gretchen Walters
Printed By: United Graphics, Inc.

Instructional Designer for the Steps to Success Activity Series: Joan N. Vickers, EdD

ISBN: 0-88011-324-3

Printed in the United States of America

10 9 8 7 6 5 4 3

Leisure Press
A Division of Human Kinetics Publishers, Inc.
Box 5076, Champaign, IL 61825-5076
1-800-747-4457

UK Office:
Human Kinetics Publishers (UK) Ltd.
PO Box 18
Rawdon, Leeds LS19 6TG
England
(0532) 504211

Contents

The Steps to Success Activity Series is a breakthrough in skill instruction through the development of complete learning progressions—the *steps to success*. These *steps* help students quickly perform basic skills successfully and prepare them to acquire advanced skills readily. At each step, students are encouraged to learn at their own pace and to integrate their new skills into the total action of the activity, which motivates them to achieve.

The unique features of the Steps to Success Activity Series are the result of comprehensive development—through analyzing existing activity books, incorporating the latest research from the sport sciences and consulting with students, instructors, teacher educators, and administrators. This groundwork pointed up the need for three different types of books—for participants, instructors, and teacher educators—which we have created and together comprise the Steps to Success Activity Series.

The *participant book* for each activity is a self-paced, step-by-step guide; learners can use it as a primary resource for a beginning activity class or as a self-instructional guide. The unique features of each *step* in the participant book include

- sequential illustrations that clearly show proper technique for all basic skills,
- helpful suggestions for detecting and correcting errors,
- excellent drill progressions with accompanying *Success Goals* for measuring performance, and
- a complete checklist for each basic skill for a trained observer to rate the learner's technique.

A comprehensive *instructor guide* accompanies the participant's book for each activity, emphasizing how to individualize instruction. Each *step* of the instructor's guide promotes successful teaching and learning with

- teaching cues (*Keys to Success*) that emphasize fluidity, rhythm, and wholeness,

- criterion-referenced rating charts for evaluating a participant's initial skill level,
- suggestions for observing and correcting typical errors,
- tips for group management and safety,
- ideas for adapting every drill to increase or decrease the difficulty level,
- quantitative evaluations for all drills (*Success Goals*), and
- a complete test bank of written questions.

The series textbook, *Instructional Design for Teaching Physical Activities*, explains the *steps to success* model, which is the basis for the Steps to Success Activity Series. Teacher educators can use this text in their professional preparation classes to help future teachers and coaches learn how to design effective physical activity programs in school, recreation, or community teaching and coaching settings.

After identifying the need for participant, instructor, and teacher educator texts, we refined the *steps to success* instructional design model and developed prototypes for the participant and the instructor books. Once these prototypes were fine-tuned, we carefully selected authors for the activities who were not only thoroughly familiar with their sports but had years of experience in teaching them. Each author had to be known as a gifted instructor who understands the teaching of sport so thoroughly that he or she could readily apply the *steps to success* model.

Next, all of the participant and instructor manuscripts were carefully developed to meet the guidelines of the *steps to success* model. Then our production team, along with outstanding artists, created a highly visual, user-friendly series of books.

The result: The Steps to Success Activity Series is the premier sports instructional series available today. The participant books are the best available for helping you to become a master player, the instructor guides will help you to become a master teacher, and the teacher educator's text prepares you to design your own programs.

This series would not have been possible without the contributions of the following:

- Dr. Joan Vickers, instructional design expert,
- Dr. Rainer Martens, Publisher,
- the staff of Human Kinetics Publishers, and

- the *many* students, teachers, coaches, consultants, teacher educators, specialists, and administrators who shared their ideas—and dreams.

Judy Patterson Wright
Series Editor

When each of us started shooting archery, we were drawn by the challenge of trying to shoot an arrow into the bull's-eye. It looked easy compared to many of the other sports we had tried. Then, when a shot would hit the bull's-eye, we'd be encouraged to keep trying. At first it was one of those fundamental tests of skill, like How far can I throw this? or How fast can I run? The more we were around archers, though, the more we could see that the challenge wasn't just to hit the bull's-eye once in a while. Rather, it was to hit the bull's-eye with EVERY shot. This was a challenge not so easily met.

We have found many ways of enjoying archery. We started shooting archery indoors at 20 yards. Just when we could shoot a good percentage of arrows into the bull's-eye, we discovered outdoor shooting and found it wasn't so easy—especially from 65 yards in the wind! Simulated bowhunting tournaments provided another challenge, that of shooting from unmarked distances. We also found a source of pleasure and pride in maintaining and adjusting our own equipment. There always seems to be something new and challenging about archery, despite its seemingly simple goal of "hitting your mark."

We have looked for ways to give back to the sport of archery some of the challenge and enjoyment we have taken from it, so writing this book was an opportunity we could not pass by. We both feel we have learned a great deal about archery through our own participation. We are teachers by instinct, desire, and profession, and we enjoy sharing this sport with others. Between us, we have taught archery at three universities and to people of all ages. Our experience undoubtedly benefits our students.

Also, we have seen many archers start off on the wrong foot, sometimes because they had no one to systematically teach them the basics, sometimes because they had no one to identify and correct their errors, and sometimes because they were handed ill-fitted equipment or more equipment than they could handle at one time. This book is an opportunity to help many archers start successfully and build on that success one step at a time.

Writing this book was a challenge, however. First, archers are not accustomed to drills as a means of learning and practicing their skills. No previously existing archery text made use of drills to the extent desired in the *Steps to Success* activity series. It was a challenge to design the drills and practice aids used in this text. We believe this unique feature will greatly contribute to your success in archery.

Second, maintaining and tuning equipment have traditionally been treated as topics for the advanced archer. We felt, however, that beginning students of archery would be interested in this phase of the sport and appreciate understanding the basic concepts of tuning a bow. It provides a working knowledge of how to improve your scoring, how to adapt to various forms of archery, and what to look for in purchasing archery equipment.

Finally, we have recognized that many archers now own compound bows or have access to them, so we have taken this into account throughout this text.

There are several people we would like to thank for their help. First, we would like to acknowledge Joan Garrison, a master teacher from whom Kathie Haywood took her undergraduate archery class. It is ideal to have a good model for archery instruction from the start. Second, we would like to thank Earl Hoyt, Jr., founder of Hoyt Archery Company, for his willingness to "talk archery" and share his vast knowledge of the sport with us. We'd like to acknowledge, too, the influence that Al Henderson's writings have had upon us. Sometimes they were the only source we could find on an aspect of shooting. Last, but not least, thanks go to Cynthia Haywood, for her help with some of the illustrations we provided the artist.

Kathleen M. Haywood
Catherine F. Lewis

The Steps to Success Staircase

Get ready to climb a staircase—one that will lead you to become a great archer. You cannot leap to the top; you get there by climbing one step at a time.

Each of the 18 steps you take is an easy transition from the one before. The first few steps of the staircase provide a foundation—a solid foundation of the basic ingredients of shooting. As you progress further, you learn how to vary your technique according to your body build and interest in various types of archery. Through your practicing, you will learn to choose the proper technique, equipment, and mental preparation to increase your shooting accuracy under various shooting conditions. As you near the top of the staircase, the climb eases, and you'll find that you have developed a sense of confidence in your archery ability that makes further progress a real joy.

To prepare to become a good climber, familiarize yourself with ''Archery From the Stone Age to the Space Age,'' ''Basic Equipment,'' and ''Preparing Your Body for Success'' for an orientation and in order to understand how to set up your practice sessions around the steps.

Follow the same sequence each step of the way:

1. Read the explanations of what is covered in the step, why the step is important, and how to execute or perform the step's focus, which may be a basic skill, concept, tactic, or combination of them.
2. Follow the numbered illustrations showing exactly how to position your body to execute each basic skill successfully. There are three general parts to each skill: preparation (getting into a starting position), execution (performing the skill that is the focus of the step), and follow-through (recovering to starting position).
3. Look over the common errors that may occur and the recommendations of how to correct them.
4. Read the directions and the Success Goal for each drill. Practice accordingly and record your score. Compare your score with the Success Goal for the drill. You need to meet the Success Goal of each drill before moving on to practice the next one because the drills are arranged in an easy-to-difficult progression. This sequence is designed specifically to help you achieve continual success. The drills help you improve your skills through repetition and purposeful practice.
5. As soon as you can reach all the Success Goals for one step, you are ready for a qualified observer—such as your teacher, coach, or trained partner—to evaluate your basic skill technique against the Keys to Success Checklist. This is a qualitative, or subjective, evaluation of your basic technique or form, because using correct form can enhance your performance. Your evaluator can tailor specific goals for you, if they are needed, by using the Individual Program sheet (see the Appendix).
6. Repeat these procedures for each of the 18 Steps to Success. Then rate yourself according to the directions in the ''Rating Your Total Progress'' section.

Good luck on your step-by-step journey to developing your archery skills, building confidence, experiencing success, and having fun!

Archery From the Stone Age to the Space Age

When you pick up a bow to shoot your first arrow, you are partaking in an activity dating back at least twenty thousand years. The bow and arrow are pictured in drawings that old on a cave wall in Spain's Valltorta Gorge.

The bow and arrow were once critical to humankind's survival. The bow allowed humans to become proficient hunters. Prey provided various raw materials—such as hide, bone, and sinew—for tools, shelter, and clothing and added more protein to the diet. It was safer to hunt with a bow, because prey could be shot from a distance.

Empires rose and fell through use of the bow and arrow as weapons. The ancient Egyptians first established the bow as a primary weapon of war around 3500 B.C. They made bows almost as tall as themselves and arrowheads of flint and bronze. Around 1800 B.C. the Assyrians introduced a new bow design: a short composite bow of leather, horn, and wood with a recurved shape. It was more powerful than the longbow used by the Egyptians and could be handled easily on horseback. This gave the Assyrians an edge in battle over their Middle Eastern rivals. The Hittites also used the short recurved bow in mobile warfare by shooting from the light, fast chariots they developed around 1200 B.C.

Middle Eastern superiority in archery continued for centuries as the peoples of this area successfully fought Europeans. For example, the Romans, although known as mighty soldiers, used an inefficient draw to the chest in shooting the bow and were outclassed as archers by the third-century Parthians of Asia. The Mongols conquered much of Europe, and the Turks threw back the Crusaders, in part because of archery equipment of the superior, recurve design and better shooting technique.

In the eleventh century, the Normans developed a longbow that they used along with superior battle strategy to defeat the English at the Battle of Hastings in A.D. 1066. Thereafter, the English adopted the longbow as their major weapon and abandoned their Saxon-style bow, which was weaker and less accurate. Many ballads of the thirteenth and fourteenth centuries, such as the tales of Robin Hood, attest to the archery skill the English developed with the longbow.

The value of the bow as a war weapon declined swiftly after the invention of firearms in the sixteenth century. But, the fun and challenge of archery guaranteed its continued existence as a sport. King Henry VIII promoted archery as a sport in England by directing Sir Christopher Morris to establish an archery society, the Guild of St. George, in 1537. Roger Ascham published the book *Toxophilus* in 1545 to preserve much of the archery knowledge of the time and to maintain interest in archery among the English. Archery societies were founded throughout the 1600s, and the tournaments they often formed firmly established archery as a competitive sport. The Ancient Scorton Silver Arrow Contest was first held in 1673 in Yorkshire, England, and continues to be held today. Women joined the men in competition and were first admitted to an archery society in 1787.

On the North American continent, Indians relied on the bow and arrow for hunting. Indian bows, however, were crude and weak; the hunter had to get close to prey to be successful. European settlers brought their well-developed knowledge of bowmaking from their native countries and kept interest in target archery alive. The first archery club on this continent, the United Bowmen of Philadelphia, was established in 1828.

Oddly, greater interest in archery in the United States was spurred by the Civil War. When the war ended, the victorious Union prohibited former Confederate soldiers from using firearms. Two brother veterans, Will and Maurice Thompson, learned archery with the help of Florida Indians. Maurice wrote a book, *The Witchery of Archery*, which helped spread interest in archery across the country. By 1879 the National Archery Association was founded and began holding national tournaments. Enthusiasm for field archery—a target archery competition simulating hunting—and hunting itself led to establishment of the National Field Archery Association in 1939.

Archery first became an official Olympic event at the Paris Olympics in 1900, an appropriate sanctioning because the mythical founder of the ancient Olympics was Hercules, an archer. Archery continued to be shot at the 1904 St. Louis Olympiad and the 1908 Olympics in England, but did not reappear until 1920 when the Olympics were held in Belgium. Archery failed to appear in any of the Olympic Games held over the next 52 years.

The problem with early archery competition was the lack of a universal set of rules. The host country had usually held the type of archery contest most popular in that country. If archery was not popular in the host country, the event was not even held during athletic meets.

To better organize competitive archery, Polish archers worked to establish an international governing body during the 1930s. As a result the Federation Internationale de Tir a L'Arc—known by its acronym, *FITA*—was founded. FITA set up universal rules and a type of round that was eventually adopted as the round shot by men and women in the modern Olympics. International competition so grew and gained momentum in succeeding decades that archery was readopted for the 1972 Olympic Games.

Technical advances in bow and arrow design have spurred shooting accuracy and, consequently, interest in archery. None has had more impact than H.W. Allen's invention of the compound bow in 1966 in Missouri. The compound bow makes use of eccentric (off-center axle) pulleys or cams, mounted in the tips of the bow limbs, to reduce the holding weight of the bow for a given draw weight. These types of bows are popular in North America for target and field archery as well as hunting. While Olympic competition is limited to the traditional, recurve bow, many archers enjoy the challenge of combining mechanical advantage and personal skill with the compound bow.

SHOOTING TARGET ARCHERY

Competitive target archery can be shot in many different types of *rounds*, or contests, unlike most sports where a single set of rules governs play. For example, indoor contests are usually shot at a single, short (20 yards or meters) distance at a single size target. Each outdoor contest, though, is usually shot at various distances with targets of variable size, depending on the distance. Some rounds call for three or four different shooting distances, whereas others require ten or more.

The number of arrows shot in a round also varies. Indoors, 30, 45, or 60 shots is typical, but 56-144 shots per round is common outdoors. Tournaments can consist of one or more rounds. Sometimes different types of rounds are shot within the same tournament.

One thing is common to all the various rounds: The scores of arrows are totaled, and the archer with the highest point total wins the contest. Unless the round simulates hunting, a target of concentric circles is used; the closer an arrow lands to the center of the target, the more points awarded.

Competitive target archery is also shot with a variety of bows, although archers are often separated into classes within a tournament or into different tournaments based on their equipment. The traditional recurve bow consists of a handle riser section made of metal, often magnesium. The bow limbs are usually composites of wood and fiberglass or plastic. An adjustable sight is mounted on the bow, as are one or more rods called *stabilizers*, that reduce the tendency of the bow to turn about its long axis upon release of the arrow (see Figure I.1a).

Figure I.1a An archer using a recurve bow in target competition.

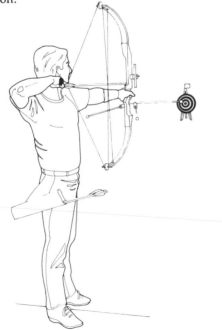

Figure I.1b An archer using a compound bow and mechanical release in target competition.

The compound bow also has a metal handle riser, but its limbs may be composite or solid fiberglass (see Figure I.1b). Eccentric pulleys or cams are mounted on the limb tips. Steel cables are attached to the pulleys, and the bowstring, in turn, is attached to the cables. A compound bow can also be equipped with adjustable sights and stabilizers.

The target arrow is usually made of aluminum or a combination of aluminum and carbon. It is equipped with a steel tip that is bullet-shaped. Real feathers or plastic vanes are attached to the rear end of the arrow. It is very important in modern target archery that all of an archer's arrows be identical in size, weight, and length.

Competitive target archery is shot with sophisticated equipment. Yet, the variability of a novice's accuracy is often due more to basic form and technique than to equipment. A simple, one-piece, traditional bow and wood or fiberglass arrows are sufficient for learning the basic techniques of archery.

SHOOTING RULES

The various archery associations, kinds of equipment, and types of rounds lead to variations in archery rules. It is important that you be familiar with the specific set of rules that govern any class, range, or contest in which you participate. Many of the rules are similar, however, and here we establish a set of common archery rules for shooting and scoring that will suffice for your early experiences in archery. Later, we will establish a set of safety rules that you must learn thoroughly.

1. If you shoot with a class or at an indoor range, the shooting distance will be specified. If there is a shooting line, stand with one foot on each side of the line when shooting.
2. There will be an established number of arrows to be shot at one time. In archery this is called an end. It is discourteous to shoot more than this number of arrows.
3. If you are shooting with a group, there may be someone assigned to control

shooting with a whistle: One blast signals the beginning of shooting; two blasts indicate archers may go forward to the target to score and collect arrows; four or more blasts indicate that all shooting must immediately cease. If there is no one to control shooting thusly, be sure to wait until all archers have finished shooting before you go forward to retrieve your arrows.

4. Archery targets can be of various types, depending on the kind of round shot. Arrows in the official five-colored, 10-scoring ring target face count as follows from the center out: 10, 9, 8, 7, 6, 5, 4, 3, 2, 1 points.

5. If an arrow touches two scoring areas on the target face, even just touching the dividing line, the higher score counts.

6. If an arrow drops from the bow as you are nocking, drawing, or letting down, that arrow can be reshot provided you can retrieve it without leaving the shooting line. If you cannot reach it, wait to retrieve it, rather than walking out in front of the shooting line.

7. If you shoot at an outdoor range, shoot from the same distance as any other archers already shooting when you arrive, unless you can leave an open target between your target and those of the other archers.

ARCHERY TODAY

Archery is enjoyed today by thousands of people all over the world. One of the reasons for its popularity lies in the many ways to enjoy archery, including target shooting and hunting. Archery can be shot by men and women, children and older adults, and by the handicapped.

Target Archery

Target archery has been popular since the days of King Henry VIII of England. The challenge of hitting your mark is timeless. Today, many archers enjoy target archery using the equipment rules established for the modern Olympic Games. The bow is limited to the recurve

style. Bowsights are permitted and the bowstring must be drawn and held with the fingers. The National Archery Association in the United States sponsors competition for archers using this equipment.

The National Field Archery Association and the Professional Archers Association in the United States allow the compound bow to be used in target competition. Bowsights with magnification and illumination are permitted. There is also an equipment class that allows archers to use a mechanical triggering device to hold and release the string. Archers in this classification may well shoot a perfect score in a round, all arrows landing in a tie-breaking x-ring within the bull's-eye.

Field archery associations usually add equipment classifications for target competition that require equipment similar to that used for hunting. The number of fixed sight pins and, therefore, sight settings is limited, as are aiming aids. The arrows must be of the type used for hunting, with a target tip installed rather than a broadhead, though.

Other Types of Archery

Bowhunting is a popular activity today. Bowhunters enjoy the challenge of taking game as they help to control the size of game populations whose natural predators have dwindled. The amount of game taken during a season is usually regulated. The majority of bowhunters now use compound bows, making hunting more humane because a kill is more likely than a wound with the increased speed and potential for heavier draw weight that the compound bow affords. The compound bow also allows smaller persons to hunt with the necessary bow draw weight.

Hunting has become so popular that bowhunters often hold competitive rounds in the off-season. Silhouette or three-dimensional styrofoam targets are placed in wooded areas at unmarked distances. Equipment is often limited to that used for hunting.

Bowfishing is another way to enjoy archery. Fish are shot from a boat or canoe with an

arrow attached to fishing line. A special reel is mounted onto the face of the bow. The fish taken are often carp, gar, buffalo, suckers, redhorse, stingray, and skates. Most effective shots are taken through a depth of 4 feet or less because water quickly slows an arrow.

Flight shooting is yet another type of archery enjoyed in some parts of the continent. Arrows are shot for distance. Special bows and arrows are usually designed for just this purpose. Today's flight bows shoot over 900 yards.

Novelty shoots are occasionally held for enjoyment and variety. These contests sometimes take the form of clout shooting, wherein a 48-foot target is laid out on the ground and shot at from 140-180 yards. Archery golf is a game shot similar to golf, with a flight arrow, an approach arrow, and a putting arrow shot at a 4-inch ball. In roving, a small group of archers take turns calling out a target to see who can come the closest.

Crossbow competition is enjoyed in some parts of the North American continent. Technical advances in crossbow design and in

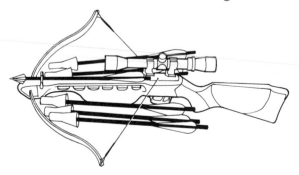

materials have made crossbows very accurate. Today's shooters aim for 60-centimeter target faces from distances as great as 65 meters.

No matter which form of archery or what type of equipment you come to enjoy, it is the same basic form and shot-to-shot consistency that leads to shooting accuracy. The equipment and your physical and mental skills must come together to produce the perfect shot.

Before you begin shooting, you should learn the various terms associated with archery *tackle*, or equipment, including the parts of the bow, the parts of an arrow, and shooting accessories. This will help you understand the directions given in the steps to archery success.

THE BOW

There are two types of bows commonly in use. One uses the bow limbs themselves to store the energy that will propel an arrow. The other stores energy in an off-center pulley or cam and is known as a *compound* bow. Of the first type, you will probably encounter two variations in an instructional setting. One is a *straight-limbed* bow made of solid fiberglass (see Figure E.1), and the other is a *recurved-limb* bow made of laminations of wood and fiberglass (see Figure E.2).

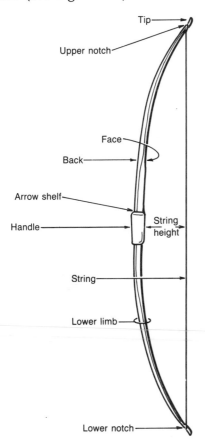

Figure E.1 A straight-limb fiberglass bow.

Straight-Limb Bows

Advantages

- Inexpensive
- Can be fitted for both right-handers or left-handers

Disadvantages

- Little cast
- Not center-shot

The straight-limb fiberglass bow is inexpensive, and the same bow can be used by both right-handed and left-handed shooters. However, the straight-limb design does not provide very much leverage when the limbs are bent by your pulling back the bowstring. The arrow sits to the right or left of center of a straight-limb bow, and you must compensate for this when aiming.

Recurve Bows

Advantages

- Greater cast
- Greater arrow speed
- Interchangeable limbs if take-down style

Disadvantages

- Shooting for distance requires high draw weight

The recurved-limb design is the most efficient one. A recurve bow has limb tips that are bent back away from you in its relaxed position. The bowstring lies across 2-3 inches of the limb. Yet, when the string is drawn back (see Figure E.2c), the curves straighten to provide leverage when the string is released and the curves return to their C-shape. This imparts more arrow speed than a straight limb. The length of the limbs is fitted for an archer's size to maximize the leverage provided by the limbs. This quality is called *cast*. The terms used to describe the various parts of both straight-limb and recurve-limb bows are given in Figures E.1 and E.2.

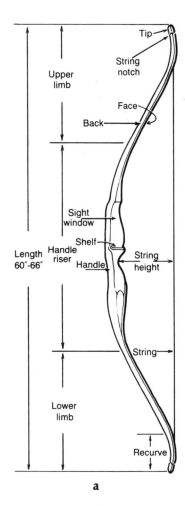

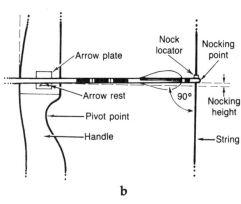

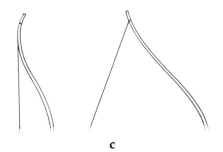

Figure E.2   A recurve bow.

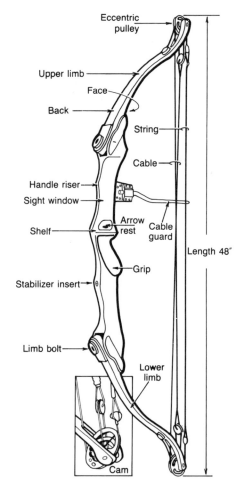

Figure E.3   A compound bow.

Compound Bows

Advantages

- Holding weight is less than draw weight
- Potentially faster arrow speed

Disadvantages

- Must be fitted for archer's draw length

Compound bows are characterized by an *eccentric*, or off-center, pulley or cam mounted on each limb tip (see Figure E.3). The energy required to rotate the part of the pulley with the long radius is greater than the energy required to rotate the part with the short radius. The pulleys are mounted so that the energy required to pull back the bowstring is the greatest at mid-draw and the smallest at full draw, when the archer is holding to aim. When the string is released, this situation is reversed and the energy applied to the arrow is actually increased. For example, an archer with a 40-pound compound bow of 50% let-off, or reduction, holds only 20 pounds of resistance at full draw; 40 pounds of thrust, however, are imparted to the arrow.

THE ARROW

There are four types of arrows commonly found on the market today: wood, fiberglass, aluminum, and aluminum-carbon. The basic terminology used to describe the parts of an arrow is the same for each type and is given in Figure E.4. Using arrows of proper length is absolutely critical from a safety perspective. Step 1 tells you how to determine your correct arrow length.

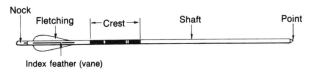

Figure E.4 Parts of a target arrow.

Wood Arrows

Advantages

- Inexpensive

Disadvantages

- Cannot be precisely matched to each other
- Not readily matched to archer's draw length and weight
- Break easily

Wood arrows are acceptable for beginning archers because they are inexpensive, but they are not very durable, and they easily warp. Because of differences in the pieces of wood used to make arrows, they cannot be closely matched. As a result, you may find variation in arrow flight from arrow to arrow.

Fiberglass Arrows

Advantages

- Can be sized to draw length and weight
- Can be better matched than wood

Disadvantages

- Break easily

Fiberglass arrows are more durable than wood, and they can also be sized to fit archers of varying arm length and strength. Fiberglass arrows of a given size can be manufactured more consistently than wood. However, they do break easily.

Aluminum Arrows

Advantages

- Can be precisely manufactured
- Wide range of sizes available
- Durable
- Arrow tips can be interchanged

Disadvantages

- Expensive

Aluminum arrows can be manufactured so that arrows of a given size meet the same specifications and, consequently, are more consistent and accurate than wood or fiberglass arrows. You can therefore purchase additional arrows at any time to match your originals precisely. Aluminum arrows are manufactured in a wide variety of sizes and in different qualities of aluminum alloy. Bent arrows can be straightened, and damaged arrow points easily replaced, so a good set of aluminum arrows can be maintained for lasting use. Although they are more expensive, their consistency and durability make them the arrow of choice.

Aluminum-Carbon Arrows

Advantages

- Speed

Disadvantages

- Very expensive
- Carbon layer breaks down if struck

Aluminum-carbon arrows are made of an aluminum core wrapped with carbon. They are smaller and lighter than pure aluminum arrows. However, they are extremely expensive and are usually used only by archers shooting long distances outdoors. They tend to be impractical for archers who tightly pack their arrows in a target, as typically happens when shooting short distances, because the carbon wrapping breaks down when struck by another arrow.

ACCESSORIES

There are several accessories required to make shooting comfortable and more accurate. One is an arm guard worn on the forearm of the hand holding the bow. It provides protection from the bowstring in case the string slaps the forearm upon its release. It also minimizes the effect on the bowstring and arrow flight should such contact occur. Several styles are shown in Figure E.5.

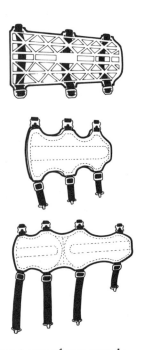

Figure E.5   Three types of arm guards.

Another valuable accessory is a finger tab, worn over the fingers that hold the bowstring. It both protects the fingers and improves the smoothness of the bowstring's release. Various finger tabs are pictured in Figure E.6.

Figure E.6   Three types of finger tabs.

A quiver is a handy accessory for holding or carrying arrows. It comes in a variety of styles (see Figure E.7). Most archers use a belt quiver. In an instructional setting, it may be convenient to use a ground quiver that is stuck into or set on the ground.

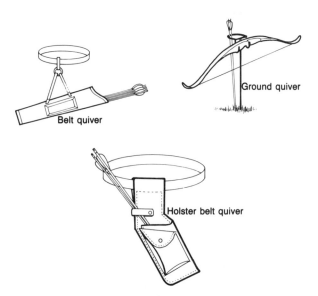

Figure E.7   Three types of quivers.

Another important accessory is an arrow rest. An arrow rest is mounted on the bow above the bow shelf (see Figure E.3). The arrow is placed on the arrow rest and remains there until it is shot. The advantage of an arrow rest over shooting an arrow off the bow shelf is that the rest allows the fletching of the arrow to clear the bow more smoothly on its flight toward the target. This allows for smoother arrow flight and, consequently, more accurate shooting.

Preparing Your Body for Success

Archery requires repetitive movement against a great deal of resistance. In other words, the same back and arm muscles contract on every draw to bring the string back to the anchor position and to hold it there. Because these muscles are working against resistance they are strengthened, but not stretched, in drawing, holding, and releasing the bowstring. In contrast, the opposing muscle groups are stretched in shooting, but never strengthened. With months of repetitive shooting, this could lead to the archery muscles shortening or tightening and their counterparts lengthening or loosening. A regular program for upper-body, arm, and shoulder stretching and muscle strengthening offsets these tendencies.

Additionally, some beginning archers already have muscles that are tight and inflexible due to poor posture or a lack of training for flexibility. This tightness makes it difficult for the new archer to use proper alignment of the body and limbs in shooting. A program of stretching and strengthening can help the archer achieve better body alignment in shooting and to do it more comfortably.

The warm-up program that follows can both prepare you for practice or competition and, in the long term, improve your flexibility and strength for shooting.

WARM-UP

Do 1 or 2 minutes of vigorous activity before stretching. This warms up the muscles and reduces the likelihood of injuring them during stretching. Jumping jacks are recommended here because they are vigorous, can be done in a small space, and involve shoulder joint movement. You can substitute rope jumping, jogging, or some other vigorous activity.

Jumping Jacks

From a standing position with your arms at your sides, jump to a side-split position as the arms swing sideways to overhead. Keep your elbows straight so that when your hands touch overhead, your arms have moved through a large range of motion at the shoulders. Jump back to a standing position, swinging your arms down to your sides. Perform the jumping jacks continuously.

STRETCHING

Stretch slowly into position, rather than bouncing, when doing a flexibility exercise. Hold each stretched position for a count of 10 before returning to the starting position. Breathe normally. If time permits, repeat each of the flexibility exercises several times.

The Hug

Cross your arms in front of your chest and put your hands on your shoulders. Slowly stretch your hands around the shoulders as far toward the middle of the back as possible. Hold this position for a count of 10 and return to the starting position. The hug stretches the muscles in your back.

Arm Circles

Slowly rotate your arms, elbows straight, in the largest circle possible. Exercise both arms, one at a time or together. Make 10 revolutions forward, then 10 backward. Arm circles stretch the muscles in the shoulder area.

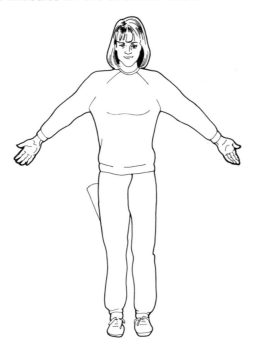

The Arm Stretch

Take a standing position. Interlock your fingers with your palms out. Now extend your

arms straight overhead, trying to keep the interlock and point your palms upward. Hold this position for a count of 10 and return to the starting position. The arm stretch loosens the upper arm and chest muscles that pull your arms down to your side.

The Hand Clasp

In a standing position, interlock your fingers, palms together behind your back. Bend your elbows to move your hands to your right, left arm against your trunk. Gradually pull your shoulders down and your shoulder blades down and together. Hold for a count of 10, then switch to your left side. Hold this position for a count of 10 and return to the starting position. The hand clasp stretches the muscles in the front of your chest.

The Up-and-Down Hand Clasp

From a standing position, bend your right arm behind your back and place the back of your right hand on your spine. Keep your shoulder down. Extend your left arm up, bend it at the elbow, and attempt to touch your right hand or even to grasp the fingers of your right hand. Keep your spine straight throughout. Hold this position for a count of 10, then reverse your arms and hold for another count of 10. If you cannot touch your hands together at first, try to stretch as far as possible until you develop the flexibility to touch. This exercise loosens your front chest muscles and those on the top of the shoulder of your lower arm.

Trunk Twister

Interlock your fingers, palms together, in a standing position. Twist your shoulders and trunk as far to the right as possible. Hold this position for a count of 10, then twist to the left. The trunk twister stretches the trunk muscles.

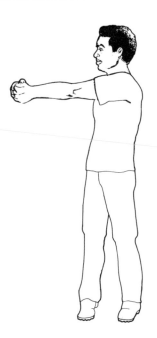

The Neck Stretch

Tip your head as far to the right as possible and hold. Stretch to the left, hold, then return to normal. Keeping your chin in, slide your head forward and hold. Then slide your head back and hold. Be sure to keep your chin level; avoid rolling your head to the back from the side position or tilting your head back. The neck stretch loosens your neck and upper chest muscles.

STRENGTHENING

Drawing and steadying a bow requires upper-body strength. Moreover, maintenance of good shooting form over an extended number of shots requires strength. Weak archers often let their form break down as they tire, resulting in a loss of accuracy. Many people find that their arms and shoulders are their weakest body parts. If this is true for you, it can be beneficial to good shooting to increase your upper-body strength. The preferred way to increase muscle strength is through a program of progressive resistance exercises. You can consult a text on strength training for more information on such a program.

Below, however, are arm exercises you can do with a piece of surgical or rubber tubing 1/4-inch in diameter and approximately 4 feet long providing resistance. This can be very helpful for competitions where the number of practice arrows before scoring begins is limited. Also, regular and frequent use of these exercises can contribute to upper-body strength. The tubing can easily be carried with you. You can do these exercises prior to shooting whether you are at an indoor range or out in the woods.

Back Pull

Grasp an end of the tubing with each hand. Keeping your elbows straight, raise your arms sideways to shoulder level. Extend your arms backward by squeezing your shoulder blades together, the tubing stretching across your chest. Relax your arms forward, then repeat the pull 4 more times. This exercise strengthens the same muscles used to draw the bowstring.

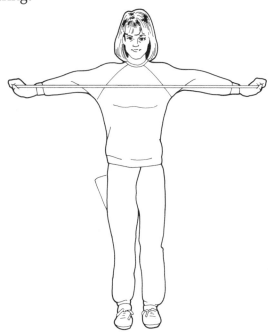

Chest Pull

Grasp an end of the tubing with each hand as above, then swing the tubing over your head and behind your back. Hold your arms straight out to the sides at shoulder level and swing them forward as the tubing pulls across your back. Relax your arms backward, then repeat the pull for a total of 5 repetitions. The chest pull strengthens the muscles that oppose the archery drawing muscles.

Frontal Plane Pulls

The movements in the following pulls are done in the frontal plane, the imaginary plane that would divide your body into front and back. Grasp an end of the tubing with each hand and raise your arms straight overhead.

Stabilizing your left arm, pull your right arm down toward your side as far as possible. You may have to tip your head forward. Return your right arm about to shoulder level, stabilize it, and pull around and down with your left arm. Repeat this exercise 4 times from the start, then reverse it. These pulls strengthen the muscles that raise and lower the arms at the shoulders in the frontal plane.

Archery Draw Pull

Grasp both ends of the tubing in your bow hand to form a loop. Raise your bow arm as if to shoot and set your draw hand hook on the loop. Pull to your anchor position, taking care to relax your biceps and use your back muscles. Repeat 10 times, relaxing between pulls. This exercise obviously strengthens the muscles used in shooting.

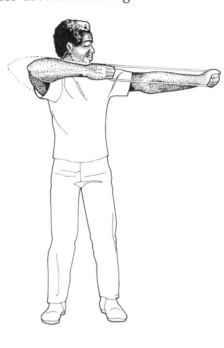

Step 1   Fitting Basic Equipment

Archery equipment must be fitted to your size and strength. In this step, you first determine whether you should shoot right-handed or left-handed. Then you figure out your draw length, bow size, and arrow size in a series of exercises. Finally, you learn to string straight-limb and recurve bows. At the conclusion of this step is a checklist for recording the equipment sizes you need to shoot archery successfully and safely; fill in the checklist as you complete each exercise in this step.

EYE DOMINANCE

Your first step in fitting a bow is to determine your eye dominance, to see whether you are same-side dominant (dominant eye and dominant hand on the same side of your body) or cross-dominant. The typical archer lines up the dominant eye with the target. If you are same-side dominant, you can shoot with a right-handed bow if you are right-handed (with your right eye dominant) or a left-handed bow if you are left-handed (with your left eye dominant).

If you are cross-dominant—that is, your left eye is dominant but your right hand is dominant or with right eye and left hand dominant—you have a choice to make. You can shoot on the side of your dominant eye, or, if you are physically more comfortable shooting on the side of your dominant hand instead, you can learn to shoot with your dominant eye closed. For example, if you are right-handed, you would close your dominant left eye to aim. Otherwise, lining up your left eye with the target while shooting right-handed may cause you to shoot your arrows to the left.

Exercise 1: One of the simplest ways to determine eye dominance is to place one hand over the other so that a small hole is created between your thumbs and fingers (see Figure 1.1). Extend your arms toward a target. With both eyes open, center the bull's-eye in the opening made by your hands. Slowly bring your arms toward your face while continuing to look at the bull's-eye with both eyes open. When your hands touch your face, the opening should be in front of your dominant eye.

An alternative method is to assume the same position, but, instead of moving your hands toward your face, keep your arms extended. With both eyes open, center the bull's-eye in the opening. Then close your left eye. If the object remains in view, you are right-eye dominant; if not, you are left-eye dominant.

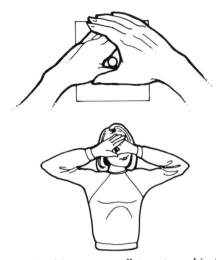

Figure 1.1 Looking at a small target or object across the room with both eyes open, the archer brings the small opening in the hands back to the dominant eye.

DRAW LENGTH

You need a draw length measurement to fit both the bow and arrows.

Exercise 2: To measure draw length, stand about 8 yards from a target with a light-poundage bow and a long arrow. If you are shooting right-handed, hold the bow in your left hand (if shooting left-handed, hold it in your right hand). Hook onto the middle of the bowstring with the first three fingers of your shooting hand. Raise the bow and pull the string back until it touches your chin. Ease the string back. Practice this several more times, making sure your bow-holding arm is fully extended.

Now snap the arrow onto the bowstring beneath the nock locator and place the arrow on the arrow rest of the bow. Pointing the bow toward the target, draw the string back. Have someone mark the arrow directly above the arrow rest (see Figure 1.2). Measure from the nock slit to the mark, as shown in Figure 1.3. This measurement is your draw length.

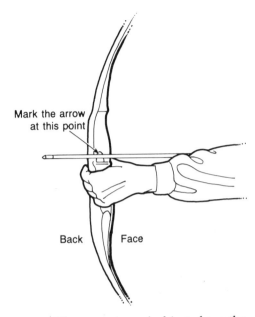

Figure 1.2 The arrow is marked just above the arrow rest after the archer comes to full draw.

Beginners often obtain an initial draw length that is slightly shorter than the length they obtain later, after they have shot for several weeks. Being new to drawing a bow, they have not yet learned to stretch as far as they should. If you decide to purchase your own equipment after your beginning archery lessons, remeasure your draw length.

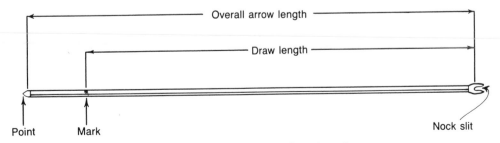

Figure 1.3 The distance from the nock slit to the mark is the draw length.

THE BOW

If you are shooting with a recurve bow, you now need to select a bow that is of proper length and weight.

Exercise 3: First, determine the bow length ideal for you by using your draw length to find the proper bow length in Table 1.1.

Table 1.1 Selection of Bow Length

Draw length	Bow length
Under 24 inches	60-64 inches
25-26 inches	65-66 inches
27-28 inches	67-68 inches
29 inches or more	69-70 inches

Exercise 4: Next, choose a draw weight. It is better to start with a light weight that you can pull and easily hold while developing good form. Keep in mind that the draw weight printed on the bow is the draw weight at a standard draw length. Older bows list their draw weights measured at 28 inches from the bowstring at full draw to the back of the bow. Newer bows list their draw weights measured at 26 1/4 inches from the bowstring to the arrow rest (see Figure 1.4).

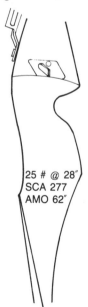

25 # @ 28"
SCA 277
AMO 62"

Figure 1.4 The draw weight of a bow at a standard draw length is printed on the bow.

If your draw length is shorter than the standard, the resulting lower string tension means you will be shooting fewer pounds than the weight stated on the bow. If your draw length is longer than standard, you will be shooting more pounds than the weight stated. In order to estimate the actual bow weight you will be shooting, you can add or subtract approximately 2 pounds for every inch your draw length is above or below the standard, respectively. You can also have the exact poundage at any draw length measured at a pro shop with a bow scale (see Figure 1.5).

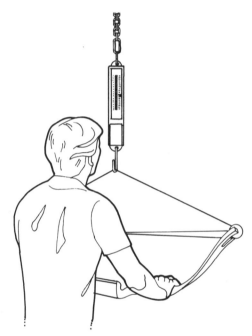

Figure 1.5 The exact draw weight of a bow can be measured on a scale.

Adult archers of average strength typically begin with a bow 20-25 pounds in weight. Stronger archers can begin with 25- to 30-pound bows. Lighter bows of 15-20 pounds are appropriate for young archers.

Compound bows must be fitted for draw weight and draw length, rather than bow length. The holding weight of a compound bow, the force that is held at full draw, is a fraction of its peak weight, the force that is imparted to the arrow. Therefore, you can select a compound bow of higher draw weight than a recurve bow. You must pull through the peak weight of a compound bow in order to reach the holding weight, so you must have the strength to pull through the peak weight.

The size of the eccentric pulley determines the point in the draw where the holding weight is reached. This point is called the *valley*. Ideally, the valley corresponds to your draw length. Many compound bow pulleys today allow an adjustment of approximately 3 inches in draw length. This makes it easier to fit a compound bow.

THE ARROW

It is important to use arrows of proper length. It can be dangerous to draw a short arrow past the arrow rest. On the other hand, an arrow that is too long does not fly well.

Exercise 5: As a beginner, you should determine your arrow length by adding at least 3 3/4 inches to your draw length. When more consistent form is established, you won't need such a large margin of safety; you can then use arrows 2-3 inches shorter.

Arrows also vary in shaft size. The rationale for determining the ideal size is presented in Step 18. For now, you can select the size of your arrow shaft from Table 1.2 if you are using fiberglass arrows, or from Table 16.1 if you are using aluminum arrows. To select a fiberglass arrow from Table 1.2, find the weight of your bow, adjusted for your draw length, in the first column. Read across to your draw length column to find your ideal shaft size. Select arrows to shoot that have this number printed on the sides of their shafts. Be sure every arrow in your set is of the same size. Notice that aluminum arrows have a

four-digit number printed on the sides of their shafts, as shown in Figure 1.6. As a beginner, having arrow shafts of the exact size specified is less important than using arrows of a safe length. You must learn good, safe form first because form is a bigger variable in your beginning accuracy than is the optimum flight of the ultimately ideal arrow.

Easton X7®	**1916**
Easton X7®	**1914**
Eagle	**1816E**

Figure 1.6 The arrow shaft size is printed on the side of the shaft.

ACCESSORIES

The fitting of accessories should not be overlooked, because they are designed to protect you and make shooting enjoyable.

Exercise 6: The arm guard is worn over the forearm of your bow arm. The fit should be snug but not uncomfortable (see Figure 1.7). You may find it desirable to use a longer style arm guard that covers the upper arm as well as the forearm.

Finger tabs are worn over the first three fingers of your draw hand. They come in right-handed or left-handed styles as well as sizes

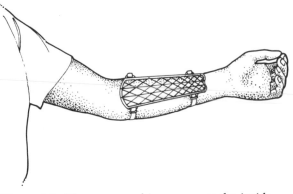

Figure 1.7 The arm guard is worn over the inside of the bow arm.

Table 1.2 Shaft Sizes for Fiberglass Arrows

Bow weight at draw length (pounds)	Draw length (inches)								
	23	24	25	26	27	28	29	30	31
20-25	0	0	0	1	2	3	4	5	6
26-30	0	0	1	2	3	4	5	6	7
31-35	0	1	2	3	4	5	6	7	8
36-40	1	2	3	4	5	6	7	8	9
41-45	1	2	3	4	5	6	7	8	9

of small, medium, and large. You should choose the size that covers your fingers without extending beyond your fingertips. Place your middle finger through the tab so that the tab lies flat against the pads of the fingers with its smooth or hairface side up (see Figure 1.8).

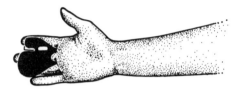

Figure 1.8 The finger tab covers the pads of the fingers used to hook onto the bowstring.

STRINGING THE BOW

Straight-limb and recurve bows are best unstrung when not in use, particularly over periods of a week or more. If left in the strung position for an extended period of time, a bow's limbs can weaken. If you are using a straight-limb or recurve bow, you should learn to string and unstring it.

There are a variety of ways to string a bow, but some are safer than others, both for you and for your bow. Several of the methods, with their advantages and disadvantages, are presented in the paragraphs below. One thing that is common to all methods is placing the larger loop of the bowstring around the belly of the upper limb and the smaller loop into the notch of the lower limb. Always be sure this smaller loop is seated in the notch, then slide the large loop into the notch of the upper limb as you flex the bow. Keep your face out of the way of the upper limb, in case your hand should slip or the bowstringer break. Also, always be sure that the upper loop is firmly seated in its notch before you release the flexing pressure on the bow. All that is necessary to unstring a bow is to reverse the procedures given below.

Cord Bowstringer Method

A cord bowstringer consists of a length of cord with a small leather pocket on each end, into which the limb tips slip. This type of stringer is safe and easy to carry. To use the cord stringer, hold the bow facedown to the ground with your left hand if you are right-handed (if left-handed, transpose directions). Place the large leather pocket on the lower limb tip and the smaller pocket on the upper tip. The cord is now hanging underneath the bow. Step on the middle of the cord with your left foot. Pull up on the bow just until the cord is taut, so that you can make sure the cord is routed underneath the bow and not alongside the limb tips. Now pull up on the bow with your left hand as your right hand slips the upper loop up the limb and into the notch, as seen in Figure 1.9. Keep your fingers on the sides of the limb so they are not caught between the bow and the bowstring. When you are sure the loop is securely seated in the notch, you can relax pressure on the bow and remove the stringer. Check the lower loop seating, too.

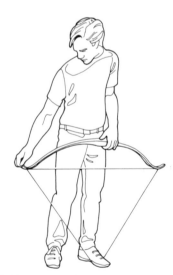

Figure 1.9 To string a bow with a cord stringer, one hand pulls up while the other slides the string loop into position.

Wall Stringer Method

Permanent indoor shooting facilities often have a bowstringer mounted on the wall. This is handy and—because you stand behind the bow during stringing—safe. It also minimizes twisting of the bow limbs. To use this stringer, the lower limb tip is placed under the stringer's bottom fixed spool and the bow handle is on its upper, movable spool (see Figure 1.10). Standing behind the bow, pull the upper limb back while sliding the upper bowstring loop up the limb and into the upper notch. Be careful not to catch your fingers between the bow and bowstring. Once you are sure the upper loop is properly seated, release your pressure slowly. Also check for proper seating of the lower loop.

Figure 1.11   One hand pushes down on the bow positioned in the box stringer as the other slides the string loop into position.

Step-Through Method

The step-through method requires no special stringer. However, there can be a tendency to twist the lower bow limb in the process of stringing the bow, so it is not the preferred method of stringing. Some archers also find the method difficult. To use this method, hold the bow vertically, its face to the left (remember to transpose these and following directions if you're left-handed). Step between the string and face of the bow with your right leg. Position the lower limb tip over the front of your left ankle and the bow handle behind your right thigh (see Figure 1.12). Your left heel

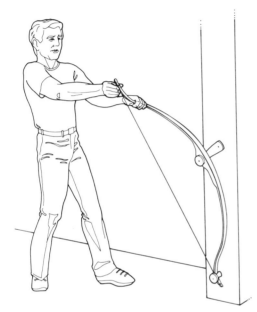

Figure 1.10   With the bow positioned in the wall stringer, the archer pulls straight back with one hand to flex the bow and slides the string loop into position with the other hand.

Box Bowstringer Method

A box stringer is safe for your bow and easy to use, although it is somewhat bulky for the individual archer to transport. The bowstringer has two arms. The movable arm should be adjusted so the recurve portion of each limb lies on an arm (see Figure 1.11). The bow is placed on the stringer face up with the upper limb to the left. The upper loop should be as far up the limb as possible. A left-handed archer pushes down on the bow handle with the right hand as the upper loop is guided into the upper limb notch with the left hand. Once both loops are checked for secure seating, pressure on the bow can be relaxed.

Figure 1.12   The bow is flexed with one hand while the other slides the string loop into position.

should be lifted slightly from the floor. Your right hand should now push the upper limb to the left, flexing the bow, while your left hand slides the upper loop into the notch. Both loops should be checked for proper seating in their respective notches.

Checklist of Equipment Sizes

Record the results of the exercises in this step so that you have a permanent record of the equipment sizes you need for shooting well and safely.

Exercise 1

Eye dominance: _____ Right

_____ Left

Bow needed: _____ Right-handed

_____ Left-handed

Exercise 2

Draw length: (#) _____ inches

Exercise 3

Bow length: (#) _____ inches

Exercise 4

Recurve bow weight: (#) _____ pounds

Adjusted bow weight: (#) _____ pounds
(Subtract or add 2 pounds per inch of draw length below or above the standard.)

or

Compound bow
   draw length: (#) _____ inches

Compound bow
   draw weight: (#) _____ pounds

Compound bow
   holding weight: (#) _____ pounds

Exercise 5

Arrow length: (#) _____ inches

Arrow shaft size: _____

Exercise 6

Arm guard: _____ Right-handed

_____ Left-handed

Finger tab: _____ Right-handed

_____ Left-handed

_____ Small   _____ Medium   _____ Large

Step 2 Shooting With Safety in Mind

Safety precedes shooting in archery. In this step you learn how to shoot safely, in order to protect both yourself and others. The safety rules are divided into those that apply before you actually shoot, those that pertain to shooting, and those to keep in mind as you retrieve your arrows. The first safety rules established here are steps to take before you actually go to the range to shoot. They are followed by safety rules that apply to shooting, then to scoring and retrieving arrows after they are shot.

WHY BE CONCERNED WITH SAFETY?

You are learning about archery as a sport; yet, you must always be aware that you hold a lethal weapon in your hand when you shoot. It is therefore important for you to learn safety rules, even before shooting your first arrow, and to follow them rigidly. Safety should be a matter for conscious attention at all times; it should never be relegated to the subconscious. Accidents often happen because people are not thinking about the task at hand; something becomes second nature to them and they no longer give it their full attention. You must shoot with safety *in mind*.

HOW TO SHOOT SAFELY

Most safety rules point out specific ways in which a bow is a lethal weapon and that you must be very careful in its use. Dangerous situations must be anticipated.

Before Shooting

Equipment Selection

1. Make sure an instructor or pro shop employee has verified that your arrows are

long enough for you. Overdrawing a short arrow is dangerous because the arrow can shatter if it lodges behind the bow; it can even embed itself in your arm (see Figure 2.1).

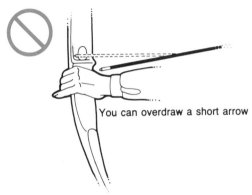

You can overdraw a short arrow

Figure 2.1 Overdrawing a too-short arrow can result in serious injury.

2. Make sure your arrows are long enough for an archer to whom you may lend your arrows.

Equipment Inspection

1. Inspect your bowstring. If it is frayed or if any strand of the string is broken, replace the bowstring.
2. Check the serving on your bowstring. If it is unraveling, tie it off, have it re-served, or replace the string.
3. Inspect your bow. If there is a crack in the limbs, do *not* shoot your bow. Have an instructor or employee at a pro shop inspect it. Otherwise, a cracked bow could break at full draw and cause an injury.
4. If you are shooting with a recurve bow, check the brace height to be sure it is at least 6 inches (see Figure 2.2). Otherwise, the bowstring may slap your wrist.

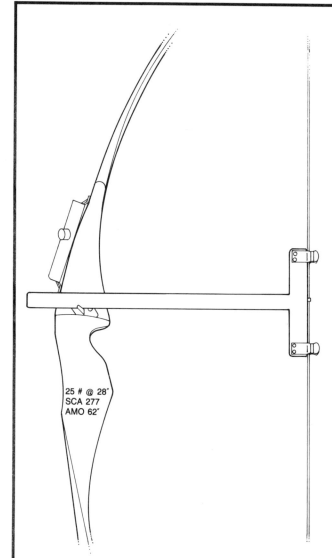

25 # @ 28"
SCA 277
AMO 62"

Figure 2.2 A bow square positioned to check the string or brace height.

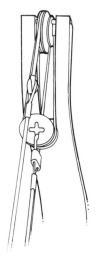

Figure 2.3 The steel cables of a compound bow should be properly seated on the pulleys.

5. Compound bows should be inspected to ensure that the steel cables are routed properly on the pulleys and that the bowstring is securely attached to the cables (see Figure 2.3).

6. Inspect your arrows. Wood arrows with cracks should be broken into two and discarded. Extremely bent aluminum arrows should be straightened before shooting. Each arrow should have a properly installed tip.

7. Inspect your arrows' nocks. Cracked nocks should be removed and replaced immediately because a damaged nock can slip off the string before release.

Attire

1. When dressing to shoot, avoid baggy shirts and sleeves, and chest pockets with buttons for trim. Remove pens and pencils from shirt pockets (see Figure 2.4). Also, avoid necklaces and pins. A bowstring could catch on any of these.

Figure 2.4 Objects should be removed from shirt pockets so that the bowstring will not catch on them when it is released.

2. If you have long hair, you may want to tie it back so that it does not become caught in the bowstring.

3. Wear shoes when shooting. Otherwise, an arrow dropped on your bare foot or stepped on in the grass could cause an injury.

4. Wear an arm guard and use a finger tab. They protect you from abrasions and blisters.

While Shooting

1. Take your position on the shooting line when instructed to do so, making sure you straddle the line so that you and all shooters are standing in one straight line (see Figure 2.5).

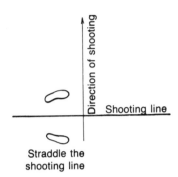

Figure 2.5 All archers should straddle the shooting line.

Figure 2.6 Never cross the shooting line to retrieve equipment, but rather rake it toward you with your bow.

2. Nock your first arrow only after the signal to shoot is given (usually one whistle blast).
3. Point a nocked arrow at the ground, or at the target butt only after the target area is declared clear. Even an arrow released from a partially drawn bow can cause serious injury.
4. Nock your arrow only at the nock locator.
5. If shooting on your own, check the target area to make sure it is clear at least 40 yards behind and 20 yards to each side of the target before each shot.
6. If an arrow falls off the arrow rest, restart the shot, rather than attempting to replace the arrow at full draw. There is the danger that you may release due to fatigue before getting the arrow into proper position.
7. Learn to shoot without holding the arrow on the bow with your index finger. You could puncture or scratch your finger.
8. If any of your equipment falls foward of the shooting line when you are shooting in a group, rake it toward you with your bow or an arrow (see Figure 2.6), rather than crossing the shooting line to retrieve it.
9. Stop shooting immediately if you hear an emergency signal. Three or more whistle blasts are often used as the emergency signal.
10. Always shoot arrows toward the target, never straight up into the air.

After Shooting

1. Step back from the shooting line when you finish shooting your arrows. However, it is courteous to remain in place if an archer next to you is at full draw.
2. Place your bow on a bow rack or in a designated area while retrieving your arrows. Someone could trip over a bow left on the ground or floor.
3. Cross the shooting line to retrieve your arrows only when given the signal to do so (usually two whistle blasts).
4. Retrieve low arrows that have landed in the grass short of the target as soon as possible on the walk to the target. If the fletching is embedded in the grass, pull the arrow forward and out of the grass to keep from damaging the fletching (see Figure 2.7).
5. Walk, rather than run, to the target and approach it with caution (see Figure 2.8). Running or tripping into the nock end of an arrow could cause a serious injury, especially to your eye.

Locate point of arrow and pull arrow through grass in the direction it is pointing

Figure 2.7 Pull an embedded arrow forward to protect its fletching.

Figure 2.9 The arrow is twisted and pulled straight back to remove it from the target butt, while the target face is anchored with the other hand.

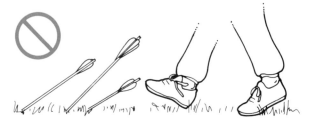

Figure 2.8 Watch for arrows embedded in the grass so you do not step on them.

Figure 2.10 Avoid eye and facial injuries by moving cautiously near the target.

6. Be sure there is no one behind you as you pull your arrows from the target. Place one hand flat against the target face to prevent it from ripping, then grasp the arrow shaft close to the target with the other hand (see Figure 2.9). Twist the arrow back and forth to remove it. This keeps the arrow from bending and avoids a large, forceful backward thrust that could strike someone nearby with the nock end of the arrow.

7. Use caution when retrieving note pads, pens, or other objects below the target. This will help prevent eye and head injuries (see Figure 2.10).

8. Be careful with arrows because the points are sharp. Carry them in a quiver or, if in hand, with the points in your palm.

9. When it is necessary to retrieve arrows behind the target, you must be sure no one else will shoot at it. One archer should remain in front of the target while the others look for the lost arrows. If you are shooting alone, leave your bow or quiver in front of the target.

Safety Test

You should demonstrate your knowledge of the safety rules of archery before shooting your first arrows. A shot arrow has more penetrability than some handgun bullets. For your sake and the sake of others learning archery with you, it is essential that you know and obey safety rules. Use the following questions to check your safety knowledge. Jot down your answer.

Before Shooting

1. What should you do if you find a crack in your bow limb?

2. What should you do if you find a crack in a wood arrow?

3. What should you do if you find a crack in the plastic nock on an arrow?

4. How should you dress for shooting?

5. For what should your bowstring be checked?

While Shooting

6. When is it safe to nock an arrow when shooting with a group?

7. When is it safe to nock an arrow when shooting on your own?

8. What does one whistle blast mean?

9. What do two whistle blasts mean?

10. What do three whistle blasts mean?

11. When is it permissible to step across the shooting line?

12. What should you do if your arrow falls off the arrow rest as you are drawing (pulling the string back) or aiming?

13. When is it permissible to hold an arrow on the bow with your index finger?

After Shooting

14. What should you do when you finish shooting your arrows?

15. How should the target be approached?

16. When should you retrieve arrows that fall short of the target?

17. When should you retrieve arrows that land behind the target?

18. For what should you check before pulling your own arrows from the target?

Success Goal = 18 correct answers. Check your answers with the safety rules. Give yourself a check mark for each correct answer. Tally and record your correct answers below.

Your Score = (#) _____ correct

Step 3   Mimicking Basic Form

Your first step toward shooting successfully is to mimic the actual shot—going through the motions of shooting, but without letting any arrows fly. In the next step, you will use the form and methods learned here to actually shoot your first arrows.

WHY IS MIMICKING BASIC FORM IMPORTANT?

You are probably eager to begin shooting. However, consider the fact that you use more equipment in archery than in most other sports. Not only must you remember how to set up and shoot with this complex gear, but you must always be aware of handling the bow and arrow safely. Mimicking gives you the chance to make the motions of shooting habitual and to get used to the equipment gradually before shooting an arrow. Mimicking contributes to safe shooting, too. You are less likely to overdraw your first arrow beyond your anchor point or have the arrow slip off the arrow rest if you have properly practiced the basic movements beforehand.

HOW TO MIMIC THE BASIC SHOT

In mimicking the basic archery shot, go through the motions of drawing the bowstring back to an *anchor position*, or anchor point— the fixed place against your body where your draw hand stops. Then ease the string back, rather than releasing it. *Never* release a bowstring from full draw unless there is an arrow in the bow, because ''dry firing'' the bow may damage its limbs.

Take a position sideways to the target. Your toes should be even along an imaginary line pointing straight to the target. Hold the bow at the grip, straight up and down in front of you. Hook onto the string with the first joints of the first three fingers of your draw hand, keeping your wrist straight and relaxed. Now raise your extended bow arm to shoulder level. Rotate your bow elbow down so that the wider portion of your arm is vertical rather than horizontal. Use your back muscles to draw the string to your anchor position by moving your draw elbow back at shoulder level. The anchor position used here places your draw hand under your chin so that the bowstring touches your nose and chin. Note that the body and arms form a T when viewed from the front (see Figure 3.1).

Figure 3.1 Keys to Success: **Mimicking Basic Form**

Stance Phase

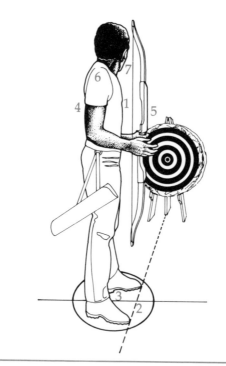

a

1. Side toward target
2. Align feet
3. Weight even
4. Stand straight
5. Bow in front
6. Shoulders square
7. Mouth closed, teeth together

Draw and Aim Phase

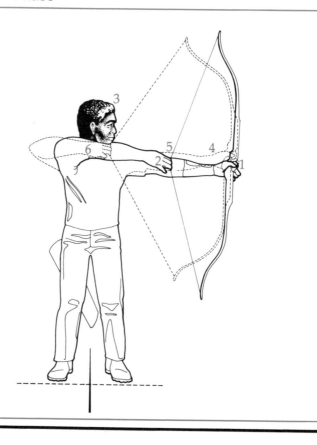

b

1. Set bow in V of thumb and index finger
2. Set string hand hook
3. Look over front shoulder
4. Raise bow toward target
5. Rotate bow elbow down
6. Relax draw hand and wrist

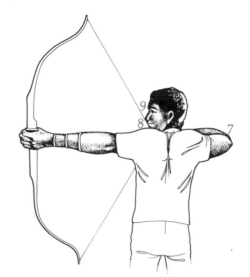

c

7. Draw elbow back at
   shoulder level
8. Chin on hand
9. String on chin and nose
10. Concentrate on target

**Release and
Follow-Through Phase**

1. Slowly ease string back

Mimicking Drills

1. Bow Arm Drill

It is helpful to practice rotating your bow elbow downward while there is pressure against
your hand. Approach a doorjamb and extend
your bow arm. Place the heel of your hand
against the doorjamb (thumb toward ceiling)
and lean against the jamb slightly. Rotate your
elbow down and around, without moving
your hand, so that the wider part of your arm
is vertical. Be sure to keep your bow shoulder down.

a

You can check your position by now bending your arm at the elbow. If your hand is at chest level, your elbow position has been correct. If your hand has ended at face level, your elbow position has been incorrect.

If you are outdoors, you can have a partner stand with arms at sides. Place your bow hand against their upper arm and practice rotating your elbow down.

b

Success Goal = 10 repetitions of rotating elbow, then checking elbow position

Your Score = (#) _____ elbow rotations with proper position

2. Shadow Drill

Standing without equipment in front of a full-length mirror, practice taking your stance, raising and extending your bow arm, and drawing to your anchor point. Concentrate on moving your string elbow straight back at shoulder level and keeping your draw wrist straight and relaxed.

Try this drill with your eyes closed, too; this makes you aware of the muscles used for the draw and the body areas that remain relaxed during the draw.

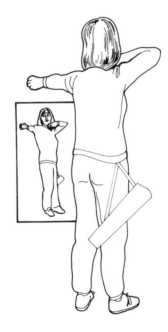

Success Goal = 10 draws without equipment, eyes open; then 10 repetitions, eyes closed

Your Score =

(#) _____ imaginary draws, eyes open

(#) _____ draws, eyes closed

3. Mimicking Drill

Standing with a bow in front of a mirror, practice setting your bow hand and a relaxed hook with your string hand fingers, raising the bow, and drawing by moving your elbow straight back at shoulder level. Keep your draw wrist straight and relaxed. Be sure to anchor with the string touching the middle of your chin and nose. Slowly ease the string back.

Also try this drill with your eyes closed.

Success Goal = 10 draws with bow, as described in the Keys to Success (Figure 3.1), eyes open; then 10 repetitions, eyes closed

Your Score =

(#) _____ draws with bow, eyes open

(#) _____ draws, eyes closed

4. Arrow Drill

Stand before a target; be sure the target area is clear. Holding a bow, nock an arrow of proper length. Practice drawing to your anchor point as described in the Keys to Success (Figure 3.1). After holding the draw for a count of 3, ease the string and arrow back.

After several draws, close your eyes while drawing the string back, increasing your awareness of using your back muscles.

Success Goal = 10 draws with arrow with proper form, eyes open; then 10 draws, eyes closed

Your Score =

(#) _____ draws with arrow, eyes open

(#) _____ draws, eyes closed

Mimicking Basic Form
Keys to Success Checklist

It is important for you to recognize in yourself as many form errors as possible. It is equally important to have someone else check you. Another person can observe you from the sides and back, and even from the front when you mimic without an arrow, to check for good alignment of your arms and trunk. The observer can also identify aspects of your shooting technique you believe you are doing properly, but in fact are not.

Have a teacher or trained observer place a check mark below in front of the "keys" they observe as you mimic a shot. You can then repeat the practice drills, emphasizing any of the keys you overlooked.

Stance Phase

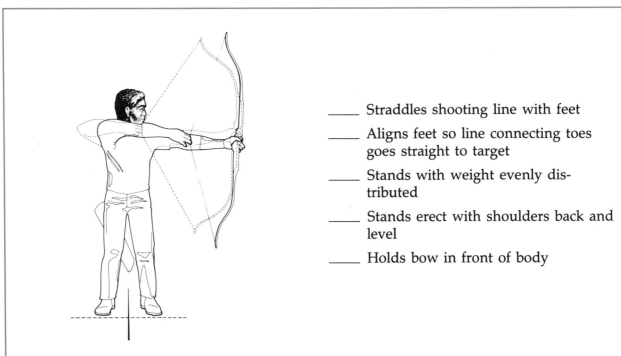

_____ Straddles shooting line with feet

_____ Aligns feet so line connecting toes goes straight to target

_____ Stands with weight evenly distributed

_____ Stands erect with shoulders back and level

_____ Holds bow in front of body

Draw and Aim
Phase

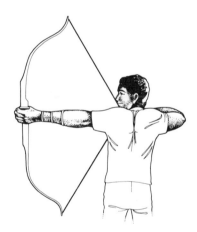

_____ Sets and relaxes bow hand

_____ Sets draw hand hook

_____ Relaxes draw wrist

_____ Raises bow, extends arm, rotates elbow downward

_____ Turns head to look over front shoulder

_____ Draws string back by moving string elbow back at shoulder level

_____ Keeps bow shoulder down

_____ Sets chin on draw hand, string touching nose and chin

_____ Tightens back muscles and holds

_____ Concentrates on target

Release and Follow-Through
Phase

_____ Eases string back

_____ Relaxes in starting position

Step 4 Shooting Form

Having mimicked the basic archery draw, you are now ready to shoot arrows. Be sure to follow the safety rules for shooting. Basic T-form is emphasized throughout this step; this is the shape formed when an archer assumes the ideal alignment of the arms at full draw with the trunk.

WHY IS BASIC *T*-FORM IMPORTANT?

Good T-alignment of the arms and trunk can be maintained by the body's muscle structure more efficiently than can other positions. Remember that in shooting archery, you maintain position for several seconds while resisting many pounds of draw weight so that you can properly aim the arrow. You may see other shooters experiencing some degree of success in shooting without perfect T-form. However, in the long run, the archer with efficient form, good basic alignment, is more comfortable and relaxed in shooting and shoots more accurately than the archer with form flaws. It is well worth the effort in your early experience with archery to make basic T-form a habit.

HOW TO EXECUTE THE BASIC SHOT

Begin your archery shot by taking the stance you did in mimicking. With the bow in front of your body, nock an arrow so that the odd-color (index or cock) feather points toward you. Set your string hand hook with your index finger above the arrow and your middle and ring fingers below it. Raise and extend your bow arm. Draw to your anchor position as you did in mimicking, tightening your back muscles. To shoot the arrow, simply relax your string hand so that your fingers no longer hold the string (see Figure 4.1).

Figure 4.1 Keys to Success: *Basic T-Form*

Stance
Phase

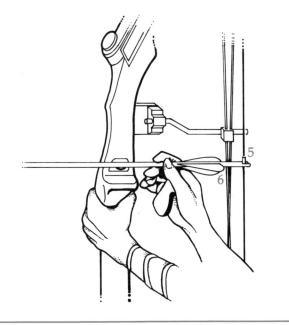

a

1. Side toward target
2. Align feet, weight even
3. Stand straight
4. Shoulders square
5. Nock arrow against nock indicator
6. Index feather toward you

Draw and Aim
Phase

b

1. Set bow hand
2. Set draw hand
3. One finger above arrow
4. Two fingers below arrow
5. Raise bow toward target
6. Rotate bow elbow down
7. Relax bow hand
8. Relax draw hand and wrist
9. Draw elbow back

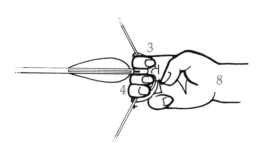

c

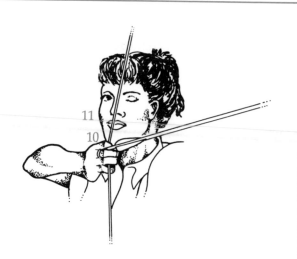

10. Chin on hand
11. String on chin and nose
12. Concentrate on target

**Release and
Follow-Through Phase**

d

1. Tighten back muscles
2. Relax draw hand to release string
3. Keep bow arm up
4. Maintain head position

Basic Shooting Drills

1. Partner Check Drill

Place a 12-inch paper plate in the middle of the target butt. Shoot an arrow from 10 yards with a partner watching. Now shoot 6 arrows (an *end*) using form as identical as possible from shot to shot. Your partner should try to catch you varying your form. You will probably find it more difficult to maintain form on your later arrows as you tire. Don't worry about striking the plate; it is only a visual focus point. Retrieve your arrows and repeat.

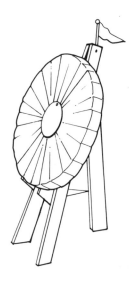

Success Goal = in each end of 6 arrows, duplicate the form used to shoot your first arrow at least 3 times

Your Score =

(#) _____ identical repetitions, end 1

(#) _____ identical repetitions, end 2

2. *Shooting Drill*

Place a 12-inch paper plate in the middle of the target butt. Shoot an end of 6 arrows from a distance of 10 yards. Don't worry about striking the plate—it is only a visual focus point. Retrieve your arrows and repeat.

Success Goal = 12 shots with form as described in the Keys to Success, Figure 4.1

Your Score = (#) _____ shots with good form

3. *Scoring Drill*

Place a piece of white paper measuring approximately 2 feet by 2 feet on the target butt. Shoot an end of 6 arrows from a distance of 10 yards and note how many land on the paper to establish a standard. Now shoot 4 more ends.

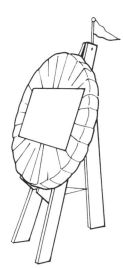

Success Goal = 4 ends equaling or bettering the number of arrows hitting paper in the standard end

Your Score =

(#) _____ arrows hitting paper in the standard end

(#) _____ arrows hitting paper, end 1

(#) _____ arrows hitting paper, end 2

(#) _____ arrows hitting paper, end 3

(#) _____ arrows hitting paper, end 4

4. Point Drill

Mount a piece of paper on the target butt as in the Scoring Drill. Draw a tic-tac-toe pattern on it with a marking pen. Write point values in the squares as shown on the pattern here. Shoot 6 arrows at a time from 10 yards. Record the number of points earned by arrows landing in squares. Arrows touching a line can take the higher point value. Shoot 5 ends of 6 arrows each.

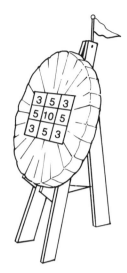

Success Goal = 4 ends with higher point totals than your first end

Your Score =

(#) _____ points, end 1

(#) _____ points, end 2

(#) _____ points, end 3

(#) _____ points, end 4

(#) _____ points, end 5

5. Target Drill

Place a traditional, multicolor archery target, 80 centimeters in diameter, on the target butt. Shoot 6 arrows at a time from 10 yards. Arrows score 10 for landing in the inner circle, 9 for the next ring, 8 for the next, and so on. Arrows touching a line can take the higher value. Shoot 5 ends of 6 arrows.

Success Goal = 4 ends with higher point value than your first end

Your Score =

(#) _____ points, end 1

(#) _____ points, end 2

(#) _____ points, end 3

(#) _____ points, end 4

(#) _____ points, end 5

6. Coin Flip Drill

Choose a partner. Shoot 6 ends in manner described in the Target Drill. Record your score on each end. Flip a coin. If heads is up, add ends 1, 3, and 5 to obtain a total score. If tails is up, total ends 2, 4, and 6. Compare your total score with your partner's.

Success Goal = to outscore your partner

Your Score =

	Heads	Tails
(#) _____ points, end 1	_____	
(#) _____ points, end 2		_____
(#) _____ points, end 3	_____	
(#) _____ points, end 4		_____
(#) _____ points, end 5	_____	
(#) _____ points, end 6		_____

Your Total: _____ or _____

Partner's Total: _____

7. Balloon Pop Drill

Blow up 6 balloons and mount them on a target butt. Shooting 6 arrows at a time from a distance of 10 yards, try to pop as many balloons as possible. When you pop them all, place another 6 on the target butt and repeat.

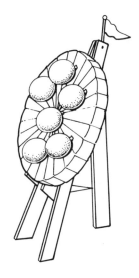

Success Goal = to pop all 6 balloons within 3 ends

Your Score = (#) _____ balloons popped in 3 ends

As you make the transition from mimicking to shooting arrows, it is important to maintain your basic T-form. It is easy to develop small flaws wherein you deviate from T-alignment without realizing it.

Basic T-Form
Keys to Success Checklist

Have a teacher or trained observer check you on the points below and indicate with a check mark which ones they observe as you shoot. You should then repeat some or all of the practice drills, emphasizing those keys you overlooked.

**Stance
Phase**

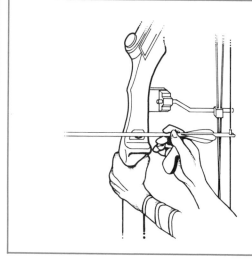

_____ Straddles shooting line with feet

_____ Aligns feet so line connecting toes goes straight to target

_____ Stands with weight evenly distributed

_____ Stands erect with shoulders back and level

_____ Holds bow up in front; nocks the arrow, cock feather toward body, against nock indicator

Draw and Aim
Phase

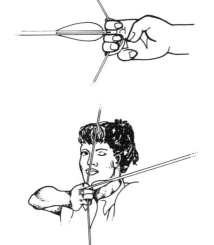

_____ Sets and relaxes bow hand

_____ Sets draw hand hook with index finger above arrow

_____ Relaxes draw hand wrist, keeps it straight

_____ Turns head to look over front shoulder

_____ Raises bow, rotates elbow down

_____ Keeps bow shoulder down

_____ Draws string back by moving draw elbow back at shoulder level

_____ Sets chin on draw hand with string touching nose and chin

Release and Follow-Through
Phase

_____ Tightens back muscles and holds

_____ Concentrates on target

_____ Holds approximately 3 seconds

_____ Relaxes draw hand to let string explode off fingers

_____ Keeps bow arm up

_____ Maintains head position, continues looking at target

Step 5   Improving Shooting Accuracy

Now that you have learned the basic form for shooting, it is time to refine your form. More attention must be given to various aspects of shooting form to achieve greater accuracy. Also, your form must be constantly monitored to correct any flaws that gradually develop as you establish the habits of shooting.

WHY REFINE YOUR BASIC FORM?

Attention is necessarily focused on a few of the basics when shooting the first arrows. Once some of these basics become second nature, the next step to success is to attend to the aspects of shooting form that have an impact on shooting accuracy. These include the bow hand, the release, and the follow-through.

HOW TO REFINE YOUR BASIC FORM

Several new details must now be added to your basic form. (Keep in mind, though, that basic T-alignment should be maintained.) One new emphasis is a bow hold that is relaxed throughout the shot. Rather than gripping the bow, form a ring with your thumb and forefinger, leaving the other fingers loose and relaxed. This minimizes the chance of moving the bow as the arrow clears, which would cause erratic arrow flight.

A relaxed string hand is also emphasized now. Your string hand merely forms a hook with the end of the fingers; the muscle force for drawing the bow comes from your back. If your wrist or base knuckles are bent, you probably are holding with your hand and arm instead of your back muscles. Back tension carries your hand backward over your draw shoulder when the hook is relaxed to release the string.

You should add a pre-draw aim to your shot, wherein the bow arm is placed at a height where the arrow tip is aligned with a spot about 18 inches below the target. After anchoring you should align the bowstring—which appears fuzzy, your aiming eye focusing on the bull's-eye—and the arrow shaft. Check the bow limbs through your peripheral vision to ensure that the bow is level. Upon the arrow's release, your head should remain stationary; your bow arm should stay up and point directly to the target. These refinements add greatly to your shooting accuracy (see Figure 5.1).

Figure 5.1 Keys to Success: **Shooting Accuracy**

**Stance
Phase**

a

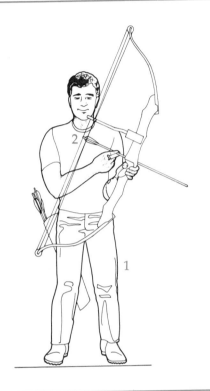

1. Assume stance
2. Nock arrow

**Draw and Aim
Phase**

b

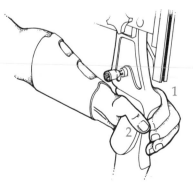

1. Set bow hand
2. Form loose ring with
   bow thumb and index
   finger

c

3. Set hook in first joints
   of fingers

d

4. Raise bow toward
   target, pre-aim

e

5. Rotate bow elbow down
6. Keep draw hand flat
7. Relax draw wrist
8. Relax bow hand
9. Draw to anchor
10. Maintain head position
11. Align string and arrow shaft
12. Level bow
13. Concentrate on target

Release and Follow-Through Phase

f

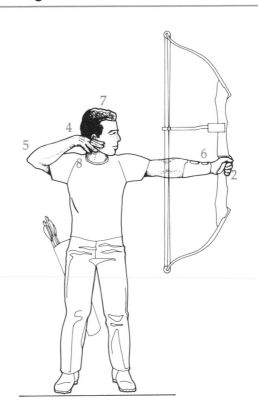

1. Tighten back muscles
2. Maintain relaxed bow and draw hands
3. Count to 3
4. Relax draw hand to release string
5. Draw elbow pulls back on release
6. Keep bow arm up, toward target
7. Maintain head position
8. Draw hand finishes over rear shoulder

Refining Form Practice Drills and Aids

1. Release Mimic Drill

Without equipment, form your draw hand hook. Hook it onto the forefinger of your bow hand and anchor under your chin. Tighten your back muscles, leaving your draw hand relaxed. Relax your fingers to "release." Your draw hand should be carried back over the rear shoulder by your back tension. This drill can be done anywhere, anytime.

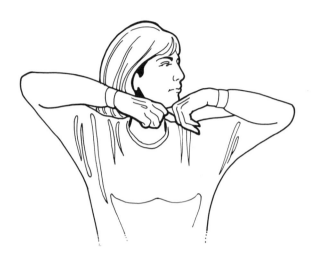

Success Goal = 9 out of 10 releases with draw hand carried back over rear shoulder

Your Score = (#) _____ releases in good form

2. Bow Hand Check

Cut two small pieces of colored tape or obtain two small dot stickers. Place one on the bow handle just above where you place your hand. Take your normal bow hand position, then place the other dot on your hand right below the one on the bow. Shoot several ends, lining up the dots on every shot to assure you take the same bow hand position.

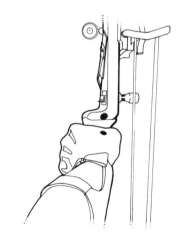

Success Goal = every shot with perfect bow hand position

Your Score = (#) _____ shots with correct position

3. Relaxation Check

Have someone observe you shoot. On 2 or 3 shots in every end, the observer should say "hold" when you reach full draw. The observer should then brush the fingers of your bow hand and the small finger and thumb of your draw hand. If they are tense, you should try to relax them. Then let down and start the shot again, taking care to relax.

Success Goal = to be relaxed on at least 2/3 of the checks

Your Score = (#) _____ relaxed full draws

4. Follow-Through Drill

Work with a partner. Shoot 2 ends as usual, but maintain your follow-through position until your partner says to relax. Instruct your partner to wait 3-5 seconds after your shot before letting you relax.

Success Goal = 10 of 12 shots maintaining perfect follow-through position

Your Score = (#) _____ shots with good followthrough

5. Grouping Drill

Experienced archers know that grouping arrows is more important than shooting occasional bull's-eyes. One can always aim at a different place to "move" the group into the bull's-eye. The scoring used in this drill emphasizes shooting a tight group of arrows.

Place any size target on the target butt. Shoot an end of 6 arrows from 10 yards. Take a tape measure to the target. Wrap the tape around all your arrows to obtain the smallest measurement possible. Record the length of tape needed to surround your arrows. This is your reference end. Shoot 4 more ends, scoring in the same manner.

Success Goal = to shoot successive ends with a smaller score than your reference end

Your Score =

(#) _____ inches, reference end

(#) _____ inches, end 1

(#) _____ inches, end 2

(#) _____ inches, end 3

(#) _____ inches, end 4

6. Symbol Target

Choose a partner. Place a large piece of paper on the target butt. With a felt marker, draw a variety of symbols—such as a square, circle, and triangle—scattered over the paper. From 10 yards, shoot 4 six-arrow ends, trying to hit the symbols. Record the number of symbols you hit below.

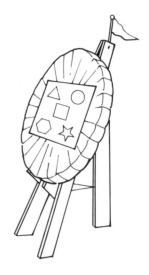

Success Goal = to hit more symbols than your partner

Your Score =

End 1: Your hits _____ Partner's hits _____

End 2: Your hits _____ Partner's hits _____

End 3: Your hits _____ Partner's hits _____

End 4: Your hits _____ Partner's hits _____

Total: Your hits _____ Partner's hits _____

7. Five-Color Shoot

Place an 80- or 122-centimeter 5-color target face on the target butt. Choose a partner. You and your partner should write the five colors of the target on five long pieces of paper or card. Shoot 4 six-arrow ends from 10 yards away. When you arrive at the target, one of you should hold the papers while the other chooses one sight unseen. For that end, double the value of any arrow in that color. Arrows cutting two colors or rings score the higher value. Pick a new color on each end. Record your score below.

Success Goal = to accumulate more points than your partner

Your Score =

End 1: Your points _____ Partner's points _____

End 2: Your points _____ Partner's points _____

End 3: Your points _____ Partner's points _____

End 4: Your points _____ Partner's points _____

Total: Your points _____ Partner's points _____

Shooting Accuracy
Keys to Success Checklist

As you attend to the more detailed aspects of shooting form, it is helpful to be checked on both the basics and the refinements. Successful shooting comes from shot-to-shot consistency. Yet, the more consistently you execute the following shot features, the more accurate your shooting will be. A check mark should be placed in front of every key that is observed by another as you shoot.

**Stance
Phase**

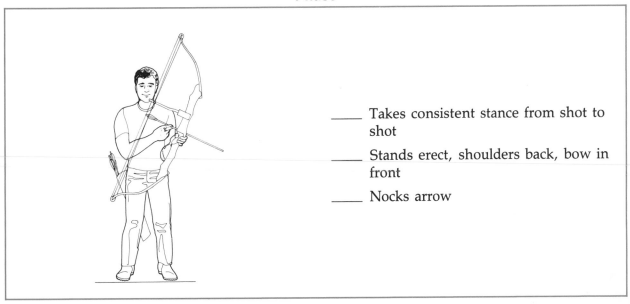

_____ Takes consistent stance from shot to shot

_____ Stands erect, shoulders back, bow in front

_____ Nocks arrow

Draw and Aim
Phase

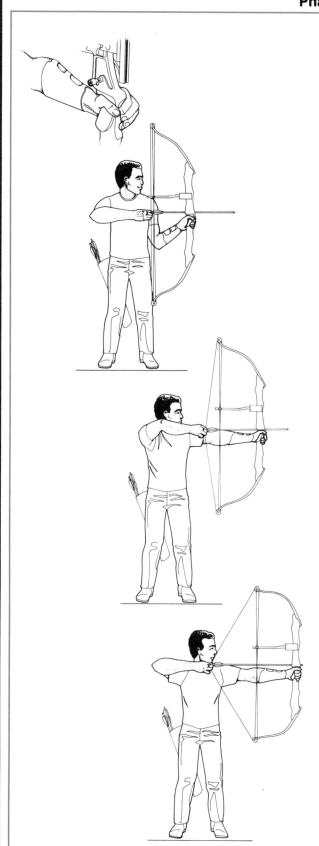

_____ Sets bow hand with loose hold

_____ Sets hook with flat, relaxed hand and wrist

_____ Raises bow, rotates bow elbow, pre-aims

_____ Draws to anchor, relaxes bow hand, maintains T-alignment

_____ Levels bow, aligns string and arrow shaft

_____ Concentrates on target

Release and Follow-Through
Phase

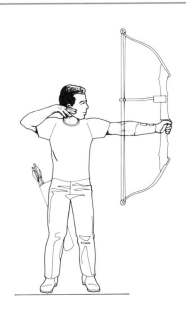

_____ Tightens back muscles while maintaining relaxed hands

_____ Counts to 3

_____ Pulls elbow back as draw hand relaxes to release

_____ Maintains position of head, bow arm

_____ Carries draw hand back over rear shoulder with back tension

_____ Identifies form errors, plans to adjust if necessary

Step 6 Adding Basic Accessories

There are several basic accessories that can improve your scoring accuracy even more, now that you have refined your basic archery form. These include a bowsight, a peep sight, a kisser button, and a bow sling. In this step, you learn why these accessories improve accuracy and how to fit and use them. They are helpful as you perfect your archery technique in your next several steps to success.

THE BOWSIGHT

The bowsight is an attachment to the bow that places a *marker*, or aiming aperture, in the bow window. You line up the aperture with the bull's-eye to aim rather than look at the relationship between the arrow and bull's-eye.

WHY IS SHOOTING WITH A SIGHT ACCURATE?

A bowsight permits you to direct an arrow to the same place, horizontally and vertically, on every shot by dictating the elevation and left/right direction of your bow arm. Moreover, if the arrow does not hit the bull's-eye at first, you can adjust the sight a known, precise amount for subsequent shots.

HOW IS A BOWSIGHT USED?

A bowsight is attached to the bow such that the aiming aperture is visible in the bow window to you at full draw, to the left of the upper bow limb for a right-handed archer. After coming to full draw, you align the aiming aperture with the center of the bull's-eye, align the bowstring with the aperture, then let the aperture steady before releasing. The sight aperture rarely stops dead, but rather settles to slow, minimal movement as you aim it. You will probably find it easier to steady your sight aperture after you acquire greater strength and muscle endurance through repetitive practice.

The aiming aperture should be adjustable both horizontally and vertically. It is helpful to have a vertical scale on the sight so that you can record the sight positions appropriate for various shooting distances. Also, if a certain sight position directs arrows slightly high or low for a given shooting distance, the scale permits you to see how much adjustment affects an arrow a given amount. Manufactured sights often come with a scale, or you can purchase an adhesive paper scale or even a short metal ruler to mount on the sight.

Target sights can be very simple, inexpensive devices (see Figures 6.1 and 6.2), or they can be elaborate, precision-made tools extended out from the bow (see Figure 18.7).

Figure 6.1 A handmade target sight with a pinhead as an aiming aperture.

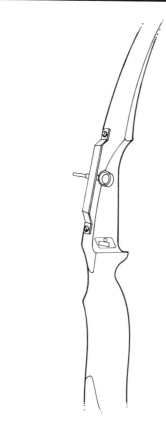

Figure 6.2 An inexpensive target sight.

Simple sights do a good job of directing the arrow as you desire. The difference between sights is typically the ease and accuracy of moving the aiming aperture.

Aiming apertures on manufactured sights can be of several types. Those apertures that are aligned with the middle of the bull's-eye include a simple post with a small round ball on the end, a ring with crosshairs, a ring with a post, and a magnifying lens with a dot in the center. Many archers prefer an open ring. They find it is natural to line up the round bull's-eye center inside the ring. Often, the various types of apertures can be interchanged on the more elaborate target sights. Some aiming apertures can also be puchased with built-in levels, but these are restricted in some equipment classifications for competition.

HOW IS A BOWSIGHT INSTALLED?

The next step to success will introduce you to shooting with a bowsight. If your bow is not equipped with a bowsight, you should install one before moving to the next step, even if it is a homemade sight.

Exercise 1: If you are able to obtain a manufactured sight, it is probably one of two types—a sight mounted flush onto the back of the bow, or one extended out from the bow on a bar or bracket. Flush-mounted sights can be installed by tapping the bow (making small holes to receive the screws) prior to inserting small screws. Drilling must be done very carefully so as not to crack the bow or weaken it structurally. Small screws should be used. If you are uncomfortable installing your own bowsight, you can have it done at a pro shop, or you can tape your bowsight tightly on your bow.

Extended sights typically come with a mounting bracket that is permanently attached to the side, rather than back, of the bow. The sight and extension bar are clamped onto the bracket for use and removed between shooting sessions. The bracket is also mounted onto the bow with screws. However, most archers choose the extended sight when using a bow with a metal handle riser that is pretapped for the sight bracket. The metal riser is much stronger than laminated wood and fiberglass and can support the weight of an extension sight.

Exercise 2: If you are unable to purchase a bowsight, you can easily make a sighting device. Obtain a 5-inch strip of foam—the type sold for insulating window and doorjambs— that is 1/2- to 3/4-inch wide. The self-stick variety is easiest to use. Place this strip on the back of your bow, even with the sight window. Cover the strip with a piece of tape upon which you can write with a permanent felt marker. Hold a metric ruler along the tape and place a mark at every half-centimeter. Number these marks from 1 to approximately 25. Obtain a long straight-pin with a ball head, and insert it into the foam so that it is visible in the sight window. You can move the pin up or down, in or out, to serve as a sight aperture.

THE PEEP SIGHT

The peep sight is a small plastic or metal disk inserted between the strands of the bowstring. It is used along with a bowsight—never alone. You look through the peep sight when aim-

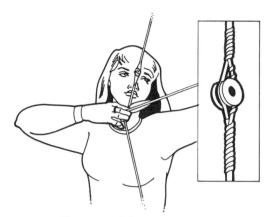

Figure 6.3 The peep sight.

ing (see Figure 6.3). Hence, it is like the rear sight on a rifle, because you are lining up a sight within a sight with the bull's-eye.

WHY DOES THE PEEP SIGHT IMPROVE ACCURACY?

In using a bowsight, you must align the bowstring with the aiming aperture as well as align the aiming aperture with the bull's-eye. Otherwise, there is the possibility that the arrow will be directed slightly left or right a varying amount on each shot. The peep sight is placed between the strands of the bowstring, eliminating the necessity of aligning the string. Moreover, it allows for more accurate alignment than possible when visually aligning the bowstring.

HOW IS THE PEEP SIGHT INSTALLED?

To install a peep sight, you should first place it between the strands of the bowstring above the nock locator at about the height of your aiming eye. Have a friend adjust it up or down while you draw and anchor in your normal place. You might also have to turn either the peep sight or the string so that the peephole is fully open to your eye; this is often a trial-and-error process. Once you have the peep sight at the correct height, you should mark the string at this location. You might also want to measure and record the height of the peep sight above your nock locator.

It is desirable to tie the peep sight into the string so that it cannot move. There are several methods for doing this, but they require prac-

tice to complete well, so you might want to take your bow to a pro shop and have an expert tie in your peep sight.

Even though you won't learn to use a bowsight until the next step to success, you are probably best advised to get used to the sight before installing a peep sight. Also, the peep sight is not allowed in some equipment classifications for competition; perhaps you should wait until you decide what type of archery you enjoy the best and what the equipment rules are for that type of archery before you install a peep sight.

THE KISSER BUTTON

The kisser button is a small disk that is attached horizontally to the bowstring above the nock locator. It is set to touch between your lips at full draw (see Figure 6.4).

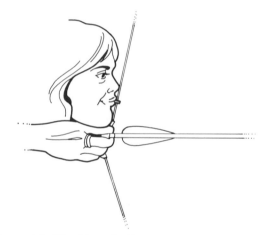

Figure 6.4 The kisser button.

WHY DOES A KISSER BUTTON IMPROVE ACCURACY?

You are already aware from the initial steps to archery success that it is important to anchor in the same location on every shot. Moving the anchor position even slightly directs the arrow off-center, even if you are using a bowsight. The kisser button aids a consistent anchor; often the kisser button does not contact your lips if your anchor position is off even slightly. Thus, you quickly realize the shot is not set up properly, and you can adjust or let the shot down and start again.

HOW IS THE KISSER BUTTON INSTALLED?

The procedure for adjusting a kisser button is much like that for a peep sight. You should slide the kisser button onto the bowstring above the nock locator at about the height of your mouth. A friend should then adjust the kisser button up or down while you hold at full draw, so that the kisser button touches between your lips. You may then want to repeat coming to full draw several times, making sure that you are using the anchor position you want. Once you are satisfied with the kisser button's location, you should mark its place on your bowstring and record its distance from your nock locator.

The kisser button should be clamped down or tied in so that it cannot move. If you decide to tie it in, it is preferable to have an expert at an archery pro shop do this for you. You can also purchase at nominal cost a small clamp that is squeezed down over the end of the kisser button with a pair of nocking pliers.

In Step 11, you will have an opportunity to try anchor positions other than the one learned in the early steps to archery success. You might want to wait until you decide in that step which anchor position you will use before installing a kisser button. The kisser button will most likely be in a different position for each of the different anchor positions. Yet, once you decide which anchor to use, the kisser button will prove to be a worthwhile addition to your archery equipment.

Most equipment rules for competition allow a kisser button. Some limit the diameter of the kisser button, and some bowhunter equipment classifications allow the use of either a kisser button or a peep sight, but not both.

Exercise 3: A kisser button is an inexpensive accessory. However, if you cannot purchase one, it is easy to make. You need a small piece of rubber (such as from a truck tire inner tube), a half-inch hole punch, an ice pick, a hairpin, and a hammer. Punch out a rubber disk with the hole punch, then use the ice pick to put a small hole in the middle of the disk. Remove the bowstring from your bow and thread it through the loop end of the hairpin to about halfway above the nock locator (see Figure 6.5). Push the hairpin and then the bowstring through the small hole in your rubber kisser button. Keep pushing the kisser button down until it clears the upper loop of the bowstring and is approximately 3 inches above the nock locator. Adjust the height of your kisser button as described above. This type of kisser button can be held in place by wrapping, then knotting, waxed dental floss around the bowstring just above and below the kisser button.

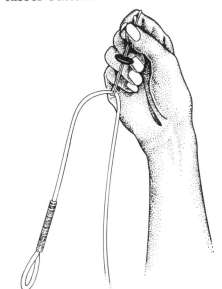

Figure 6.5   Threading a handmade kisser button onto the bowstring.

THE BOW SLING

The bow sling is a rope or strap that encircles your hand or fingers so that the bow cannot fall to the ground, even if you release your grip on the bow handle.

WHY USE A BOW SLING?

The early steps to success stressed a loose grip on the bow handle. Yet, many archers continue to grip the bow tightly because they fear dropping the bow with a loose or open hand position. A bow sling is inexpensive and allows you to relax the bow hand without fear of dropping the bow.

HOW DOES A BOW SLING WORK?

There are various types of bow slings, as pictured in Figure 6.6. Some attach to the bow;

you slip your hand through the strap when you take hold of the bow. Others attach to your thumb and forefinger or to your wrist. The type of sling you use is a matter of personal preference. All of them work well, and their expense is small in comparison to the improvement in shooting accuracy that is gained with a relaxed bow hand.

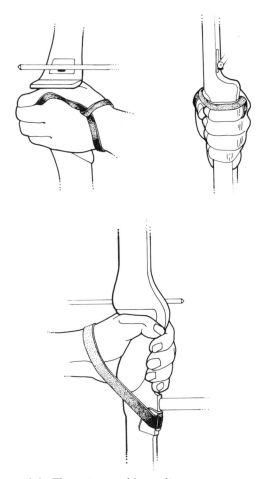

Figure 6.6   Three types of bow slings.

Exercise 4: The type of sling that wraps around your wrist is inexpensive, but you can make one yourself, if you prefer. You need a 24-inch piece of nylon cord, a candle, and a lanyard hook. If you have a small hand, cut

your nylon cord to 20 inches. Melt the ends of the cord with the candle flame to keep them from fraying. Tie a slip knot with one end of the cord to form a loop big enough to fit over your hand (see Figure 6.7). Slip the lanyard hook over the other end of the cord and bend the small end of the hook to leave a quarter-inch opening. Slip the large loop over your bow hand and grip your bow. Bring the free end of the cord around the bow handle, between your fingers, and hook it onto the cord at the inside of your wrist. Tie in the lanyard hook at the place that makes the bow feel secure in your hand but allows you to relax your hand.

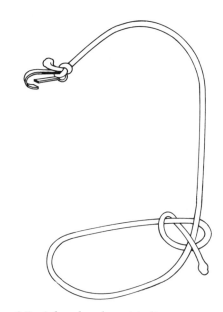

Figure 6.7   A handmade wrist sling.

In Step 10, you will have an opportunity to experiment with several variations of the bow hand position. It is desirable to begin using a bow sling by that time so that you can give your full attention to perfecting your bow hand position.

Step 7 **Sighting and Aiming**

Your shooting has undoubtedly become more accurate as you have refined your shooting form. This accuracy results from good technique and consistency of form from shot to shot. Now you can achieve even greater accuracy by using a bowsight. Although some archers enjoy the challenge of shooting without a bowsight, the majority of archers use a sight regardless of whether they are target shooting or hunting, and whether using the traditional recurve bow or a compound bow. It is preferred over every other aiming technique. In this step, you learn how to aim with, and adjust, a bowsight.

WHY DOES A BOWSIGHT IMPROVE ACCURACY?

A sight makes it possible to direct your arrows to the same spot on the target from shot to shot. If your arrows hit outside the bull's-eye, you can use the sight as a calibrated means of adjustment for subsequent shots. This adjustment can be made in either, or both, the horizontal and vertical directions; you must previously establish through trial and error just how great an adjustment is needed. When you change shooting distance, move the sight vertically—down for a greater distance, up for a shorter distance. A lower sight requires you to hold the bow higher to align sight and bull's-eye, directing the arrow in a higher trajectory to compensate for a longer distance. The horizontal adjustment allows you to accommodate slight changes in shooting form that direct the arrow to the right or left, and to adjust for shooting conditions, particularly wind.

HOW TO USE A BOWSIGHT

The principles of using a bowsight are the same whether you have a simple, homemade sight or a sophisticated tournament sight. You aim the sight aperture at the bull's-eye on every shot. The shooting form you refined in previous steps remains the same when using a bowsight, but several key points related to aligning the sight must be added to your shot. After anchoring, align the sight aperture and bull's-eye using the eye on the draw-hand side of your body. Remember that if your other eye is dominant, you may need to close it so that you use only the draw-side eye for aiming. Level the bow, then adjust your head position so that you see the string running down the middle of the bow. The string should be just to the right, for a right-handed archer, of the aperture (see Figure 7.1). Your eye should bring the bull's-eye clearly into focus, permitting the aperture and bowstring to blur slightly. Let the sight aperture steady in the middle of the bull's-eye. This usually takes several seconds. When it is steady and aligned, tighten your back muscles and relax your draw hand to release the string.

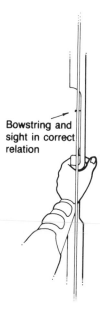

Bowstring and sight in correct relation

Figure 7.1 Proper alignment of the string with the aiming aperture.

You will be able to hold the sight more steady as you practice and develop greater muscle strength. However, archers can rarely stop the aperture "dead" in the bull's-eye; attempting to do so usually results in too much tension in the bow and draw hands.

If you are using a peep sight, rather than aligning the string as described, you should look through the peep sight and make sure the bull's-eye is centered in the opening.

You establish the proper horizontal and vertical position of the aiming aperture by trial and error. After you shoot several arrows, ob-serve their location on the target face. Move the aperture in the direction of error. That is, if the arrows group low, move the sight aperture down; sighting through a lower aperture results in your holding your bow arm and, consequently, your bow higher. If the arrows group high, move the sight aperture up. If the arrows group right, move the aperture to the right. If the arrows groups left, move the aperture left. Be sure to make left/right adjustments with the bowsight oriented to the target (see Figure 7.2).

Figure 7.2 Keys to Success: *Sighting and Aiming*

Stance Phase

a

1. Assume stance
2. Nock arrow

**Draw and Aim
Phase**

b

1. Set bow hand and draw hand
2. Raise bow, rotate bow elbow down
3. Draw, anchor

c

4. Close eye opposite draw side if necessary
5. Align draw-side eye with sight and bull's-eye
6. Level bow
7. Adjust head to see string bisecting bow, aligning just to right of aperture
          or
   Center target in peep sight
8. Focus on bull's-eye
9. Steady the sight aperture in middle of bull's-eye

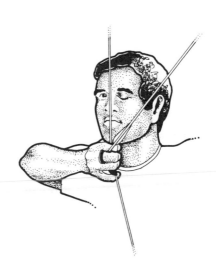

**Release and
Follow-Through Phase**

d

1. Tighten back muscles
2. Relax draw hand to release
3. Keep bow arm up, head steady

Sighting and Aiming Drills

1. Aiming Mimic

Without using an arrow, practice drawing, aligning your string and sight, and aiming from a distance of 20 yards. Aim for a count of at least 3, then ease the string back.

Success Goal = 10 repetitions of steady aiming

Your Score = (#) _____ aiming mimics

2. Sight Adjustment Practice

In this exercise you practice designating the direction of sight adjustment. The location of a group of arrows is given below in terms of a clock face. Fill in the direction(s) of sight adjustment needed to bring subsequent shot groups to the center of the target. Example: For a group at 4 o'clock, adjust right and down.

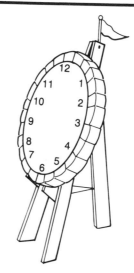

Success Goal = to make the correct sight adjustment in every situation

Your Results =

For a group at 6 o'clock, adjust _____

For a group at 8 o'clock, adjust _____

For a group at 1 o'clock, adjust _____

For a group at 3 o'clock, adjust _____

For a group at 11 o'clock, adjust _____

3. Sighting In

Shoot at an 80-centimeter target face from a short distance of 10 yards. Shoot 3 arrows, using an initial sight setting with the aperture high on the sight bar. Note where the 3 arrows land and adjust your sight. Continue shooting and adjusting until your arrows group around the bull's-eye. Record the location of this sight setting below.

Now move to 15 yards and repeat this process. When you have established a sight setting, record it. Continue this process, moving back in 5-yard increments to a distance of 40 yards.

You can anticipate the needed sight adjustment by moving your sight down a small amount each time you increase your distance from the target.

Success Goal = to establish a sight setting for every distance from 10-40 yards in 5-yard increments

Your Results =

10-yard sight setting _____

15-yard sight setting _____

20-yard sight setting _____

25-yard sight setting _____

30-yard sight setting _____

35-yard sight setting _____

40-yard sight setting _____

4. *Holding Drill*

Archers sometimes develop a tendency to release as soon as their sight is on the bull's-eye, failing to steady and aim. Put up a 3-spot target face (a target with 3 sets of the 6, 7, 8, 9, and 10 rings) or a large sheet of paper with 3 bull's-eyes drawn on it. Without shooting, stand from 10-20 yards, draw an arrow to align the string and center the sight. Once you have steadied on the first bull's-eye, move to the second bull's-eye, align, steady, and aim; move to the third, align, steady, and aim; then let down and relax. Repeat this at least 10 times. (You can let down after the second bull's-eye if you tire.)

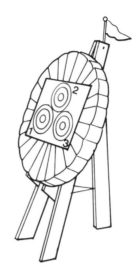

Success Goal = 10 repetitions of aiming cycle

Your Score = (#) _____ repetitions

5. *Square Target Drill*

Place a large sheet of paper on the target butt. Draw squares of the following dimensions scattered around the paper: 5 × 5 inches, 6 × 6 inches, 7 × 7 inches, 8 × 8 inches, and 9 × 9 inches. Write ''10 points'' under the smallest, ''9 points'' under the next largest, and so on. Choose a partner. Shoot continuous ends from 25 yards. See who can get to 100 points with fewer arrows.

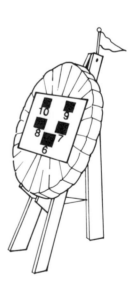

Success Goal = to reach 100 points with fewer arrows than your partner

Your Score =

    End 1: _____ points _____ arrows shot

    End 2: _____ points _____ arrows shot

    End 3: _____ points _____ arrows shot

    End 4: _____ points _____ arrows shot

6. Dart Board Game

Place a large sheet of paper on the target butt. Draw a large circle, then divide it into 8 pie slices with a felt marker. Randomly write in point values from 1-8 on each pie slice. From 20 yards, shoot 4 six-arrow ends, keeping track of your score on each end.

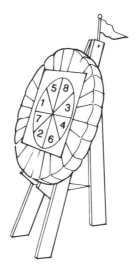

Success Goal = to improve your score on each successive end

Your Score =

End 1: _____ points

End 2: _____ points

End 3: _____ points

End 4: _____ points

7. Quick Sight Move

Place an 80-centimeter target on the target butt. Start at 40 yards and shoot a 6-arrow end. Record your score, then move to 35 yards and shoot another end. Continue moving up in 5-yard increments until you have completed an end at 20 yards. Now move back to 40 yards and repeat.

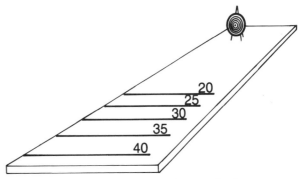

Success Goal = to score higher in the second round than in the first round at each distance

Your Score =

	Round 1	Round 2
40 yards	_____	_____
35 yards	_____	_____
30 yards	_____	_____
25 yards	_____	_____
20 yards	_____	_____
Total	_____	_____

8. Subtraction Drill

Choose a partner. Place an 80-centimeter target on the target butt. Each of you should place a piece of tape around one of your arrows. Shoot from 30 yards. On each of 4 ends, total your 5 unmarked arrows. Then subtract the value of your opponent's marked arrow from your score.

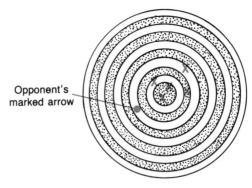

Opponent's marked arrow

Success Goal = to outscore your partner (e.g., End 1: 44 points − 7 points = 37)

Your Score =

End 1: _____ points − _____ points = _____ Partner: _____

End 2: _____ points − _____ points = _____ Partner: _____

End 3: _____ points − _____ points = _____ Partner: _____

End 4: _____ points − _____ points = _____ Partner: _____

Total: _____ Partner: _____

Sighting and Aiming Keys to Success Checklist

You now have several aspects of aligning your bowsight that must be added to your execution of the shot. The following observer's checklist emphasizes these aspects of sighting and aiming.

Stance Phase

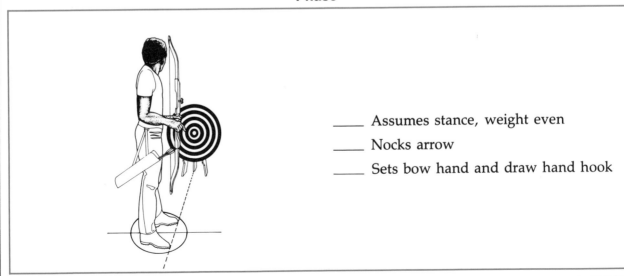

_____ Assumes stance, weight even

_____ Nocks arrow

_____ Sets bow hand and draw hand hook

Draw and Aim
Phase

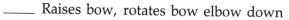

_____ Raises bow, rotates bow elbow down

_____ Draws, anchors

_____ Closes eye opposite draw side, if necessary

_____ Levels bow

_____ Gradually steadies sight in middle of bull's-eye

Release and Follow-Through
Phase

_____ Tightens back muscles, maintaining relaxed hands

_____ Relaxes draw hand to let string explode off fingers

_____ Maintains position of head, bow arm

_____ Reports draw-side eye was aligned with sight and bull's-eye

_____ Reports head position was adjusted so string bisected bow (seen just to right of aperture); or target, sight in peep sight

_____ Reports target was in visual focus

_____ Adjusts sight, if necessary

Step 8   **Detecting Errors**

Your shooting accuracy undoubtedly has improved as you refined your shooting form and learned to use a bowsight. Still, you may find that some of your shots consistently err in the same directions, or you may feel tension in a certain body area, typically resulting from shooting without proper alignment. It is valuable to know the cause of any problem in shooting technique and how to correct it. This step shows you how to detect and correct your errors by two different methods—arrow pattern analysis and technique analysis.

WHY LEARN TO DETECT YOUR OWN ERRORS?

Athletes in any sport benefit from the instructions and suggestions of knowledgeable teachers and coaches. This is especially true for archers. However, your instructor will not always be available to keep a watchful eye on your technique. You could be shooting in a tournament and have the first two arrows of an end land right of the bull's-eye. No instructor could assist you in correcting this mistake if they were not present to see your first two shots. Therefore, your remaining arrows must be shot without your teacher's help. You will shoot more consistently if you yourself can identify errors in your technique and correct them.

HOW TO DETECT ERRORS

There are two basic methods of monitoring any errors that develop in sports performance. One way is to observe the result of your performance. In archery this involves an analysis of the pattern your arrows form on the target face; form errors can cause consistent directional errors. For example, if several arrows in each of your ends land to the right

of your other arrows, any of several shooting flaws may be the cause. If all of your arrows land to the right of the bull's-eye despite repeated corrections of your sight setting, you should suspect one of these flaws in your form as the cause.

To help describe shot locations, the target face is often compared to a clock face (as in the Sight Adjustment Practice Drill in the previous step). Arrows landing to the right of the bull's-eye, for example, are described as 3 o'clock errors; arrows landing right and slightly high are called 2 o'clock errors; and so on.

The second method for analyzing performance is to observe the details of technique used. In archery the stance, draw, anchor, hold, release, and follow-through are observed for alignment, consistency, and proper execution. Obviously, you cannot watch yourself as you shoot. However, it is possible to have someone take videotapes, films, or photographs as you shoot. You can then examine your own form, not having to rely solely on someone else for an analysis.

Of course, some errors in shooting technique will be readily apparent to you—for example, the arrow falling off the arrow rest. Analysis makes you realize this is the result of curling the draw fingers—closing the hand, which twists the string to which the arrow is attached—rather than keeping the back of the draw hand flat and relaxed.

You can analyze both your arrow patterns and your shooting technique by using the tables below. You should do this periodically in order to detect and correct errors before they become habits. Later steps will address variations in archery technique. Additional analysis items related to these variations will also be presented in later steps.

Arrow Pattern Analysis

Often a technique error or equipment set-up flaw causes a consistent directional error. If you notice that a portion of your arrows land apart from the rest, or that all of your arrows group away from the bull's-eye despite repeated corrections of your sight setting, use the following chart to identify possible technique errors (if left-handed, transpose where necessary). Flaws in equipment setup are discussed in Step 16, Tuning Your Equipment.

CAUSE OF "RIGHT" ARROWS   CORRECTION

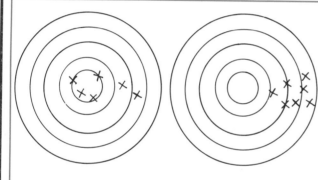

1. Bow cants to right.

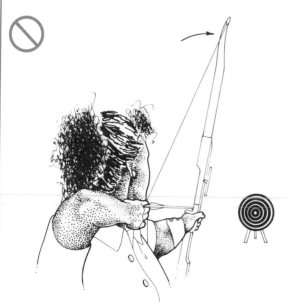

1. Before sighting, check the limbs for vertical position with peripheral vision or the level on your sight aperture.

CAUSE OF "RIGHT" ARROWS   ## CORRECTION

2. Eye lines up bowstring too far left of bowsight.

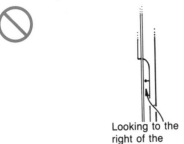

Looking to the right of the bowstring— instead of left

2. Before aiming, align the bowstring with middle of limbs and just to right of aperture (with peep sight, simply center target in sight).

3. You place bow hand too far left on handle.

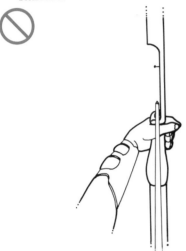

3. Place the bow hand so forearm bones directly take the force of the bow resistance as the string is drawn.

4. Bow wrist breaks left on release.

4. Relax the bow hand and wrist throughout shot.

5. Bow arm moves to right on release.

5. Relax the bow hand throughout shot and follow-through. Keep visual focus on bull's-eye until arrow lands.

6. Hand plucks bowstring on release.

6. Release the string simply by relaxing; increase back tension while aiming.

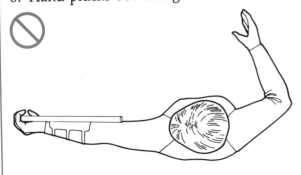

CAUSE OF "RIGHT" ARROWS   CORRECTION

7. You hold bowstring too far in on draw hand.

7. Hook the bowstring in the distal joint of fingers; keep back of hand flat.

8. You peek to watch arrow in flight.

8. Keep visual focus on the bull's-eye until arrow lands.

9. You fail to use back muscles to draw and hold.

9. Begin the draw by moving draw elbow back, keeping arm relaxed.

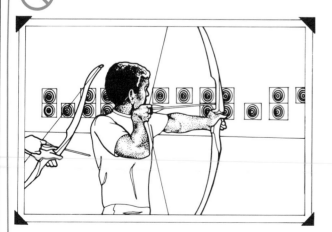

10. Body leans forward.

10. Distribute weight evenly; stand up straight.

CAUSE OF "RIGHT" ARROWS

CORRECTION

11. Stance addresses target off-center, along line intersecting target to right of bull's-eye.

11. Adjust stance so imaginary line through toes intersects bull's-eye.

12. Wind gusts left to right.

12. Adjust sight setting. Wait out strong gusts of wind before shooting.

CAUSE OF "LEFT" ARROWS

CORRECTION

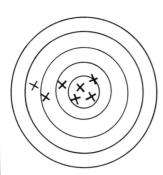 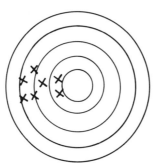

13. Bow cants to left.

13. See correction 1.

CAUSE OF "LEFT" ARROWS   CORRECTION

14. Eye lines up bowstring too far right of bowsight.

14. See correction 2.

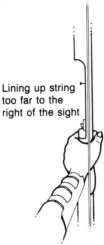

Lining up string too far to the right of the sight

15. You place bow hand too far right on handle.

15. See correction 3.

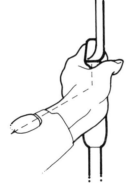

Top view

Top view

16. Bow wrist breaks right on release.

16. See correction 4.

17. Bow arm moves left on release.

17. See correction 5.

18. Hand plucks bowstring on release.

18. See correction 6.

19. Draw fingers tighten during hold.

19. Keep back of draw hand flat, draw hand relaxed.

Position of arrow while drawing if back of hand is kept flat

As the hand is cupped, the arrow tends to move with the fingers away from the arrow rest

Direction of draw

CAUSE OF "LEFT" ARROWS   **CORRECTION**

20. Draw fingers squeeze arrow nock.

20. Use snap-on nocks; place fingers above and below arrow nock; use back muscles to move bowstring.

21. Hand grips bow too tightly.

21. Relax bow hand during draw; keep it relaxed on release. If a bowsling is not used, form a ring around the bow with the thumb and forefinger to hold bow, keeping rest of fingers relaxed.

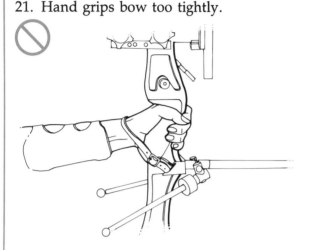

22. You nock arrow with index feather down.

22. Nock so index feather is toward you.

23. You anchor to right of normal anchor position.

23. Draw straight back to anchor position, close to bow arm. Feel the string in the middle of the chin and nose.

24. Head pushes forward during draw and anchor.

24. Hold head up; bring string back to head.

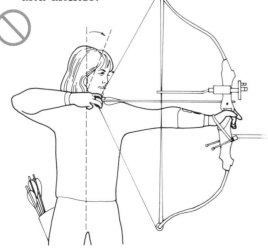

CAUSE OF "LEFT" ARROWS   **CORRECTION**

25. Bowstring hits bow arm or clothing.

25. Rotate bow elbow down before drawing. Wear tight-fitting clothes or use clothing shield. Open stance slightly (see Step 9).

26. Form collapses on release.

26. Follow through; keep visual focus on the bull's-eye until arrow lands.

27. You fail to use back muscles to draw and hold.

27. See correction 9.

28. Body leans backward.

28. See correction 10.

29. Stance addresses target along line intersecting target left of bull's-eye.

29. See correction 11.

30. Arrow slides off arrow rest (error 19).

30. See corrections 19 and 20.

31. Wind gusts right to left.

31. See correction 12.

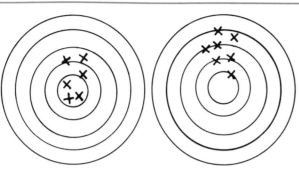

32. You anchor with jaw open.

33. You peek to watch arrow in flight (see error 8).

34. Hand "heels" bow (heel of hand pushes bow handle) at release.

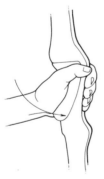

35. Arm pushes bow up on release.

36. Hand grips bow too low on handle.

37. You anchor in inconsistent location.

32. Keep teeth together.

33. Keep visual focus on bull's-eye until arrow lands.

34. Keep bow hand relaxed throughout shot.

35. Extend bow arm to bull's-eye throughout shot.

36. Move hand up; check for consistent position on every shot.

37. Use consistent anchor; use kisser button.

CAUSE OF "HIGH" ARROWS   **CORRECTION**

38. Arm draws beyond anchor position.

38. Place chin on draw hand and nose on string; also, see correction 37.

39. Nose lifts from string.

39. Place nose on string, then maintain head position throughout shot.

40. Chin drops down to anchor.

40. Keep head up, bring string to head.

41. You hold head too far back during anchor and hold.

41. See correction 38.

42. Elbow high on draw.

42. Move draw elbow back at shoulder level.

43. Elbow points downward during draw.

43. See correction 42. Also, increase back tension during hold.

44. Fingers place uneven pressure on bowstring.

44. Form hook with fingers but draw with back muscles. Bring draw elbow back at shoulder level.

45. Fingers jerk back on release.

45. Release string by relaxing fingers.

46. Fingers flick down on release.

46. See correction 45.

47. You hold bowstring too far in on draw hand.

47. Hook onto string at distal joint of fingers.

48. You inhale just before release.

48. Exhale before aiming and releasing.

49. You extend bow arm and shoulder more than usual.

49. Draw by moving draw elbow back.

50. You lean away from target.

50. Distribute weight evenly; stand up straight. Use back muscles to draw.

51. Tailwind gusts.

51. See correction 12.

CAUSE OF "LOW" ARROWS   **CORRECTION**

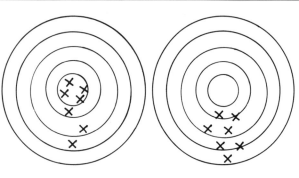

52. Creeping (moving draw hand forward from anchor).

52. Increase back tension during hold. Use clicker.

53. Bow arm drops at release.

53. Keep bow arm extended toward bull's-eye until arrow lands.

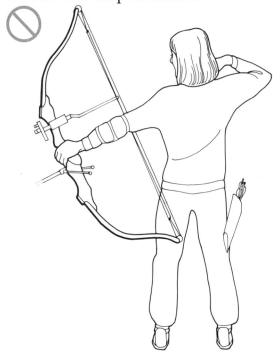

54. Bow arm bends.

54. See correction 53.

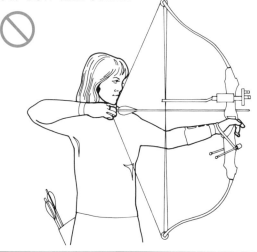

CAUSE OF "LOW" ARROWS

CORRECTION

55. Bow wrist goes to high position.

55. Relax bow hand, draw with back muscles.

56. You place bow hand too high on handle.

56. Move hand down; check for consistent position on every shot.

57. Bow shoulder comes up during draw and hold.

57. Extend bow arm toward bull's-eye, use back muscles to draw, squeeze shoulder blades together.

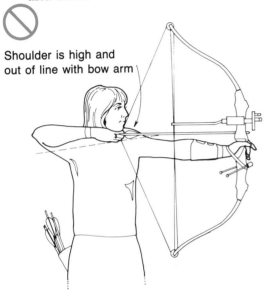

Shoulder is high and out of line with bow arm

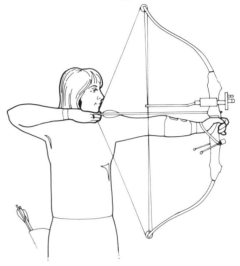

58. Head moves forward.

58. Keep head up; bring string to head.

59. You anchor higher than usual.

59. See correction 37.

60. Draw stops before reaching anchor position.

60. Bring string back to touch chin and nose.

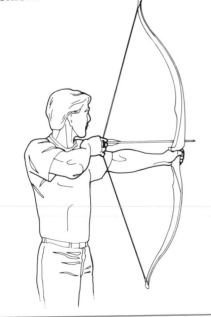

CAUSE OF "LOW" ARROWS   CORRECTION

61. Head rises on release.

61. Keep visual focus on bull's-eye until arrow lands.

62. You use a "dead release" (hand remains stationary; fingers extend to release string).

62. Increase back tension during hold so hand recoils over rear shoulder on release.

63. You fail to use back muscles.

63. Begin draw by moving draw elbow back.

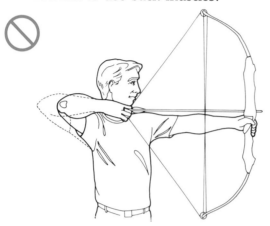

64. Draw elbow lowers at release.

64. Increase back tension during hold.

When elbow is lowered upon release it causes the arrow to go low

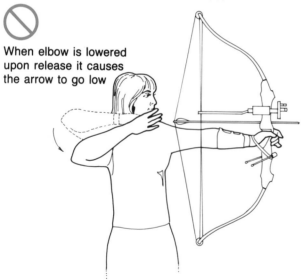

65. You draw with high elbow when using side anchor.

65. Move draw elbow back at shoulder level.

66. Tension develops in draw hand.

66. Increase back tension during hold; keep hand relaxed.

67. You lean toward target.

67. Stand up straight; bring string back to anchor position.

68. Bowstring strikes bow arm or clothing.

68. See correction 25.

69. Headwind gusts.

69. See correction 12.

CORRECTION

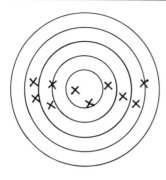

70. You use wrong eye to aim.

71. You don't align bowstring at same place on every shot.

70. Recheck eye dominance; if dominant eye is not one on draw side, close nonaiming eye; or, if this is difficult, wear eye patch.

71. See correction 2.

Technique Analysis

You can often identify technique errors in your shooting by examining videotapes or pictures of yourself. Watch carefully for T-alignment in back and front views. Watch for alignment along a line straight to the target in views from behind, looking downrange. You also may be able to feel yourself making a technique error, although archers often do not realize how they are positioning their bodies and limbs.

ERROR 🚫   **CORRECTION**

1. Hips slide toward target, upper body bends away from target.

🚫

1. Stand straight; use back muscles to draw by moving draw elbow back. Switch to bow that is lighter in draw weight if you cannot make this correction.

2. Body turns slightly to face target.

🚫

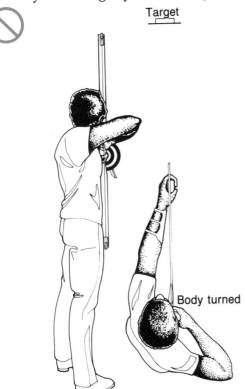

Target

Body turned

2. Check stance for foot alignment. Start with side toward target; keep shoulders square.

Target

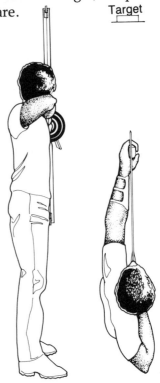

ERROR ⊘

CORRECTION

3. One shoulder is higher than other (see error 57 in ''Cause of Low Arrows'').

4. Bow and string are in front of body, rather than in line to target.

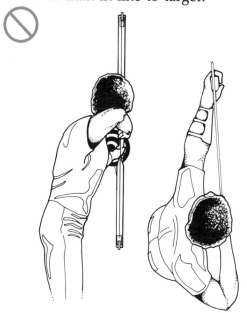

3. To begin draw, raise and push bow straight to target, then move draw elbow back at shoulder level.

4. Stand up straight, keep good posture during the draw; hold head up, level; draw string alongside bow arm.

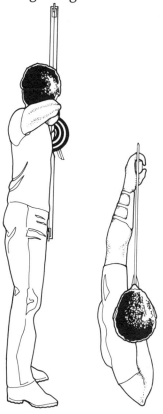

5. Draw arm points to side and back, rather than straight back.

5. Begin draw by moving draw elbow back at shoulder level; bring draw hand straight back to anchor; use back muscles.

ERROR 🚫   **CORRECTION**

ERROR	CORRECTION
6. String comes to side of face, requiring movement of head to put nose and chin on string. 	6. Slide draw hand straight back under chin; put chin on index finger of draw hand; bring string to head.
7. Arrow falls off arrow rest or bow shelf (see error 19 in ''Cause of Left Arrows'').	7. Form hook with draw hand fingers, keeping back of hand flat and relaxed. Avoid squeezing arrow with fingers.
8. String strikes bow arm upon release.	8. Rotate elbow down and out before coming to full draw. Make sure bow hand is directly behind bow handle.
9. Fingers of string hand are sore. 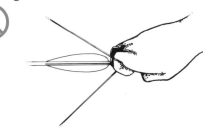	9. Make sure hand is straight up and down, not turned palm-down. Relax draw hand.
10. Bow arm is down or to side when arrow strikes target (see error 53 in ''Cause of Low Arrows'').	10. Keep bow hand pointed to bull's-eye until arrow lands, maintain relaxed bow hand.
11. Draw hand pulls away from neck upon release (plucking) (see error 6 in ''Cause of Right Arrows'').	11. Relax draw hand; tighten back muscles throughout shot; relax draw fingers to release string and allow hand to recoil over rear shoulder.
12. Bow is canted to right or left at full draw (see error 1 in ''Cause of Right Arrows'').	12. Check bow limbs with peripheral vision or level on sight before aiming.
13. Head moves to watch arrow in flight (often accompanied by moving bow arm right) (see error 8 in ''Cause of Right Arrows'').	13. Maintain head position throughout draw, aim, and follow-through; maintain visual focus on bull's-eye until arrow lands.

ERROR   **CORRECTION**

14. Release occurs before full draw is reached or before sight has steadied on bull's-eye.

14. First be sure draw weight of bow is not too heavy. Then practice aiming mimic and holding drills in Step 7 to overcome habit of quick release.

15. Bow arm elbow is bent (see error 54 in ''Cause of Low Arrows'').

15. Extend bow hand straight to bull's-eye throughout shot.

16. Head is pushed forward toward target (see error 24 in ''Cause of Left Arrows'').

16. Hold head erect; bring string back to head.

17. Draw hand turns palm-down after release.

17. Keep back tension during hold; simply relax draw fingers to release.

Practice Drills

1. Arrow Pattern Analysis

Shoot several ends from 20 yards. Before pulling your arrows, plot their locations with Xs on the targets on the next page.

When you finish, look for your most common directional errors. Review the possible causes in the ''Arrow Pattern Analysis'' lists (pp. 69-81). Write down the most likely causes for your missed shots. If your directional errors are not perfectly horizontal or vertical—for example, at 5 o'clock—check both of the closest directional errors (in this case "low" and "right"). Causes found in both tables are very likely the causes for this error.

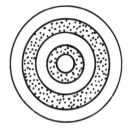 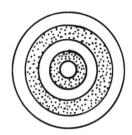 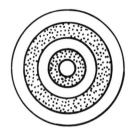

Success Goal = to correctly identify technique errors from arrow patterns

Your Directional Errors

1. _____ o'clock

2. _____ o'clock

3. _____ o'clock

Possible Causes

1. _____
   _____
   _____
   _____
   _____

2. _____
   _____
   _____
   _____
   _____

3. _____
   _____
   _____
   _____
   _____

Now choose two or three causes and list their corrections below as goals for your next practice session.

1. I will _____
   _____

2. I will _____

_____

3. I will _____

_____

Before your next practice session, review these goals. After 3 or 4 practice ends, again plot your arrows on the targets below to see whether you have corrected any of your directional errors.

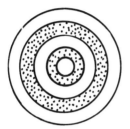 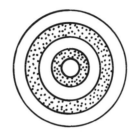 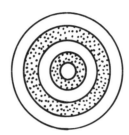

2. Picture Analysis

Have a friend take videotapes or photographs as you shoot. Ask for pictures of the following views: full body, facing you from down the shooting line; full body, from the back (pointing downrange); from your back, slightly from your bow side; close-ups of your upper body, draw/anchor hand, and bow hand. If you are working with photos, have pictures taken both at full draw and immediately after release.

Study the pictures or videotapes to identify any of the technique flaws described in the ''Technique Analysis'' section (pp. 81-85). If you have photos, it might help to draw a T right over your body on the front view photo. If you have videotapes, sketch the location of your arms, legs, and trunk over the T at the right. List below any technique errors that you find.

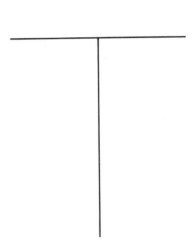

Success Goal = to correctly identify technique errors from videos or photographs

Technique Errors

1. _____

2. _____

3. _____

Now list the corrections for these technique errors as goals for your next practice session.

Goals

1. I will _____

_____

2. I will _____

_____

3. I will _____

_____

Just before your next practice session, review these goals.

3. Error Correction

Compare your list of possible causes for errors obtained in Drill 1 and the list of technique errors obtained in Drill 2. List below any flaws that appear in both lists. If there are no common errors, list the errors that violate good arm and trunk alignment.

Success Goal = to discover similar technique errors by means of two different types of analyses

Common Technique Errors

1. _____

_____

2. _____

_____

3. _____

_____

Now list corrections for these errors as goals for your next practice session.

Goals

1. I will _____

_____

2. I will _____

_____

3. I will _____

_____

Review these goals just before your next practice session. Obviously, the errors revealed by both an arrow analysis and a technique analysis are limiting the accuracy of your shooting. It is well worth the time to correct them.

Step 9 Varying Your Stance

As part of your basic form, you take a stance with your feet about shoulder-width apart and your toes along a line straight to the target. This is known as the *square stance*. It is a natural position, easy to establish, and easy to duplicate from shot to shot. Now that you have established and practiced the basic shot, you may want to consider varying your stance from this basic square stance. In this step, you learn the open and closed stances and the advantages and disadvantages of each.

WHY VARY YOUR STANCE?

The square stance is undoubtedly a good stance for beginners, largely because it is natural and easy to duplicate. However, every archer has a unique natural stance, a stance that feels the most comfortable. Your body build often dictates that one stance is better than another for you. You must experiment to find your natural stance, keeping in mind that there must still be good alignment of the upper body to maintain proper shooting form.

HOW TO VARY YOUR STANCE

The Keys to Success listed below (see Figure 9.1) show you how to assume each of the three basic archery stances: square, open, and closed. The degree and distances given are only suggestions for places to begin. You should try varying each of the basic positions to find the one most comfortable for you. Once you find your natural stance, you may want to use footmarkers to promote consistency, especially until the stance becomes second nature.

Figure 9.1 Keys to Success: *Stance*

Square Stance

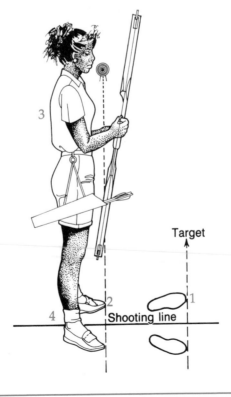

a

1. Feet apart shoulder width
2. Toes aligned
3. Body erect
4. Weight even

Advantages

- Natural position
- Easy to duplicate

Disadvantages

- Small base of support in front-to-back (sagittal) plane
- Body can sway, especially in windy conditions
- Minimizes string clearance, especially for heavy-chested shooters; string may strike clothing, chest, or upper arm on release

**Open
Stance**

b

1. Front foot turned outward 45 degrees
2. Rear foot forward 6 inches
3. Body erect
4. Rotate at waist to square shoulders
5. Weight even
6. Line to target intersects middle of rear foot, toes of front foot

Advantages

- Provides more string clearance with chest, shoulders, and upper bow arm than any other stance
- Provides stable base of support
- Minimizes tendency to lean away from target

Disadvantages

- Promotes tendency to twist upper body to face target
- Promotes tendency to use arm more than back muscles to draw

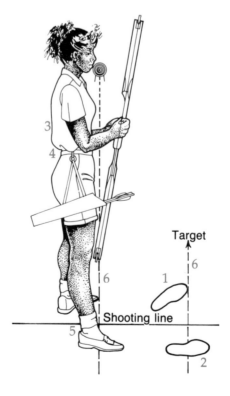

**Closed
Stance**

c

1. Front foot turned out-
   ward 45 degrees
2. Front foot forward
   6 inches
3. Body erect
4. Weight even
5. Line to target intersects
   toes of rear foot, middle
   of front foot

Advantages

- Provides stable base of
  support
- Promotes good alignment
  of arm and shoulder in
  direct line to target

Disadvantages

- Minimizes string clear-
  ance; string may strike
  clothing, chest, or upper
  arm on release
- Promotes tendencies to
  lean away from target
  and overdraw

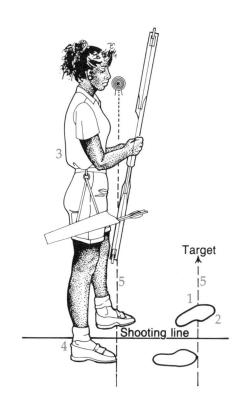

Detecting Stance Errors

Every builder knows how important it is to have a good foundation. In shooting accurately it is important to have a good base of support that allows the upper body to maintain T-alignment. Beginning archers often think that taking a stance is so simple that it is not important to check it carefully. Yet, many deviations from T-alignment can be traced back to the stance. Below are common technique errors that are often attributable to the stance, with their corrections.

ERROR

CORRECTION

1. Foot position varies from shot to shot or end to end.

2. Tension is felt in draw arm with open stance.

1. Use footmarkers: Golf tees work well outdoors, chalk or tape indoors.

2. Rotate upper body if necessary to keep shoulders in line to target.

3. You lean away from target when using closed stance.

4. Head rotates to rear, causing overdraw with closed stance.

3. Make sure weight is evenly distributed on both feet. With closed stance make sure body is erect; consider opening stance slightly.

4. Maintain head position. If using closed stance, consider opening stance slightly.

Stance Drills

1. Impact Variation

This drill demonstrates how stance influences your sight setting. Shoot an end from 20 yards to make sure you are sighted into the bull's-eye. Now shoot an end with your natural stance, then an end with a square stance. Note the center of your arrow group; estimate and record below its distance from the bull's-eye. Now shoot an end with a stance more closed than your natural stance. Again note the center of your arrow group. Shoot a final end with a stance more open than your natural stance and note the center of your arrow group.

Success Goal = to see the effect of varying the stance

Your Results =

(#) _____ inches drift, square stance

(#) _____ inches drift, more closed

(#) _____ inches drift, more open

2. Alignment Check

Stand approximately 20 yards from the target. Without actually shooting an arrow, come to full draw and place your sight pin on the bull's-eye. Close your eyes and count to 3. Open them and note whether the sight has drifted to the left or right. If it drifted to the right, open your stance a little; if it drifted to the left, close it a little (if left-handed, transpose). Correct your foot position approximately an inch at a time.

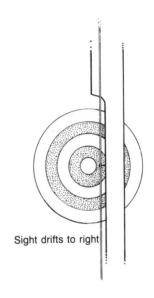

Sight drifts to right

Success Goal = 3 successive draws without drifting

Your Results = (circle) drift and correction, as needed

Draw 1
  Drift: right or left or none
  Correction: open or close stance

Draw 2
  Drift: right or left or none
  Correction: open or close stance

Draw 3
  Drift: right or left or none
  Correction: open or close stance

3. Golf Tee Drill

With two golf tees in hand, take a stance on the shooting line. Push the golf tees into the ground at your toes. Now move behind the shooting line. Sight down the golf tees to see whether an imaginary line through your stance (see Figure 9.1) goes straight to the target. Record whether or not it intersects the bull's-eye on the chart below.

   Often 3 or 4 archers shoot at a target at one time; you must learn to take a correct stance even if you cannot stand squarely in front of the target. Repeat this exercise by moving 3-4 feet up the shooting line, then 3-4 feet down the line from your first position.

Success Goal = 3 repetitions with perfect alignment

Your Score = (#) _____ correct alignments

4. Partner Stance Check

Choose a partner. Take your natural stance in front of the target from about 20 yards distance. Shoot an arrow. Have your partner stand behind you looking downrange, and sight down the imaginary line that would intersect your front and back shoulder to see whether it points to the bull's-eye as you come to full draw. Now move several feet up, then down, the line as in Drill 3 above. Have your partner check you each time.

Success Goal = 3 repetitions with perfect alignment

Your Score = (#) _____ correct alignments

5. Distance Drill

Variations in your stance affect your accuracy more at longer distances. Shoot 4 ends of 6 arrows at each of 25, 30, 35, and 40 yards distance. Use golf tees to maintain a consistent stance at each distance. Plot the 24 arrows shot at each distance with an **X** on the charts below. Look for any horizontal drift in your groups as you increase shooting distance.

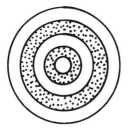 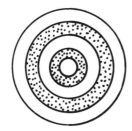 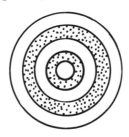 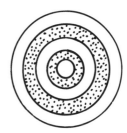

Success Goal = to maintain centering of groups at increasing distance

Your Results =

  25 yards: Drift? _____

  30 yards: Drift? _____

  35 yards: Drift? _____

  40 yards: Drift? _____

If you find that your arrows drift with increasing distance, use the golf tees as in Drill 3 above whenever you shoot from various distances until you can line up with the target perfectly at any distance, in any position.

Stance
Keys to Success Checklist

Never overlook the importance of the stance. Archers sometimes forget to duplicate their stances from shot to shot or practice session to practice session. They unknowingly introduce errors into their form because they cannot achieve T-alignment with the stance deviation. If not corrected quickly, this could become habit.

Frequently check your stance on the points listed below by having an experienced observer watch you or by having someone take videotapes or photographs so that you can check yourself. Have a check mark placed before each key observed in your shooting.

Square Stance

_____ Aligns feet so that direct line to target intersects toes of both feet

_____ Places feet shoulder-width apart

_____ Distributes weight evenly

Open Stance

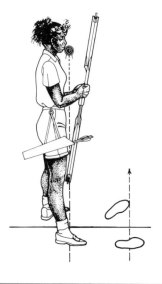

_____ Turns front foot outward 45 degrees

_____ Moves rear foot forward 6 inches

_____ Twists upper body at waist to keep shoulders in line to target

_____ Distributes weight evenly

_____ Draws so that draw elbow is in line with shoulders

Closed
Stance

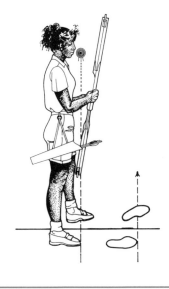

_____ Turns front foot outward 45 degrees

_____ Moves front foot forward 6 inches

_____ Keeps body erect

_____ Anchors string hand properly

_____ Distributes weight evenly

Step 10 Choosing a Bow Hand Position

You can use one of several bow hand positions: the low wrist, the high wrist, or the straight wrist. In this step you learn how to use each and how to select the one best for you. With each bow hand position, strive to maintain a relaxed bow hand such that you actually resist the push of the bow on your bow arm as the string is drawn, rather than gripping the bow. Choose the hand position that best allows maintaining a relaxed hold, given your strength and bone-muscle structure.

WHY DEVELOP A GOOD BOW HAND?

Any movement of the bow as the arrow is clearing the arrow rest can cause a deviation in where the arrow lands. Consider that pushing the tail end of an arrow just 1 degree off-center can make it land inches from the bull's-eye. You want to avoid any movement of the bow at the time of release. If your bow hand is tense or grips the bow in a tight hold, you are more likely to move upon release than if your bow hand is relaxed.

Many archers also have a tendency to grab the bow as they release the string, even if their bow hands are relaxed during draw and aiming. This *torque*, or turning of the bow, can still affect the tail end of the arrow as it clears the arrow rest. Also, it is easy to begin anticipating the release, so that the bow is actually moving throughout the release. Only dedicated practice relaxing your bow hand throughout the shot and follow-through can overcome these errors.

There is an additional reason for maintaining a relaxed bow hand. Your two hands tend to mirror one another in tension level. If your bow hand is tight, your string hand tends to be tight as well. If your bow hand is relaxed, your string hand tends to be relaxed, too, resulting in a cleaner release of the string.

HOW TO CHOOSE THE BOW HAND POSITION

The Keys to Success in Figure 10.1 explain how to use each of the three bow hand positions. The three variations put your wrist at a different height in relation to the bow hand. Regardless of which hand-wrist position minimizes torque and bow movement the best for you, there are two common features of the three variations. First, an imaginary line running down the center of the bow arm should intersect the center of the bow. This brings the line of pressure closest to the line of pressure exerted by the bowstring, making torque easier to control. Second, your hand and fingers must be completely relaxed. The bow then jumps forward to be caught by the bow sling, rather than turning to the right or left. The bowstring travels a straighter line as it accelerates the arrow, and the arrow clears the bow without interference from the bow.

Which position you use is largely a matter of preference, but you may find that your particular strength and structure lends itself to a particular bow hand position. Also, the shape of the bow's handle or grip can determine that you should use a particular position. Some bows are made with removable hand grips so that you may install the hand grip with the preferred shape. Experiment with the various bow hand positions to determine the best one for you, but remember: It is always important to maintain a relaxed bow hand throughout the shot.

Most archers grip the bow tightly because they fear dropping the bow. An inexpensive accessory that helps overcome this apprehension is a bow sling. If you have not been using a bow sling, you may want to begin using one now. The various types were explained in Step 6.

Figure 10.1 Keys to Success: Bow Hand Position

Low-Wrist Position

1. Hand on bow, pressure along inner side of thumb
2. Bow rests on base of thumb
3. Centerline of arm intersects center of bow
4. Relax wrist backward as bow is drawn
5. Relax hand, fingers

Advantages

- Allows wrist to relax backward completely
- Does not require great wrist strength

Disadvantages

- Promotes tendency to grab bow, if wrist and fingers are not relaxed

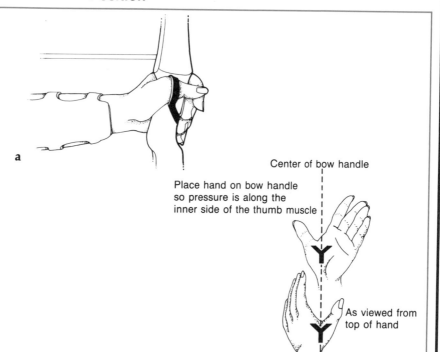

Center of bow handle

Place hand on bow handle so pressure is along the inner side of the thumb muscle

As viewed from top of hand

a

b

High-Wrist Position

c

1. Centerline of arm intersects center of bow
2. Wrist higher than hand
3. Pressure of bow on small area of hand
4. Relax hand, fingers

Advantages

- Minimizes area of hand contacting bow handle
- Minimizes bow torque
- Minimizes tendency to grab bow on release

Disadvantages

- Difficult to maintain over long shooting session without great strength
- Promotes tendency to move wrist at release with fatigue

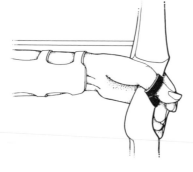

Straight-Wrist
Position

d

1. Centerline of arm intersects center of bow
2. Wrist level with hand
3. Pressure of bow on web of hand
4. Relax hand, fingers

Advantages

- Consistent from shot to shot
- Makes deviations in position easy to feel

Disadvantages

- Difficult to maintain over long shooting session without great strength
- Pressure against skin web between thumb and forefinger promotes tendency to wrap fingers around bow

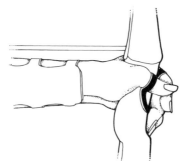

Detecting Bow Hand Errors

It is difficult to pick out any one aspect of shooting form that is more important than the others. Most expert archers would choose bow hand form if forced to make a choice. Just a small movement of the bow at release can affect the arrow, yet this movement can be almost impossible to see with the naked eye. Below are some of the common errors in bow hand technique and how to correct them, regardless of the bow hand position used. (If left-handed, transpose if necessary.)

ERROR

CORRECTION

1. Knuckles are white during hold and aim.

1. Relax fingers of bow hand.

2. Fingers are extended and locked into position.

2. Relax fingers of bow hand. Though this technique can appear to keep hand from gripping bow, it puts tension in bow hand, and you may grab bow at release anyway.

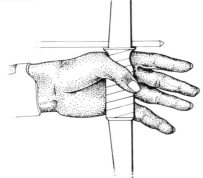

3. Wrist slides around to right of handle for right-hander. String may then slap wrist (see Step 8, error 15).

3. Place hand so centerline of arm intersects center of bow.

4. Wrist goes to left of handle for right-hander (see Step 8, error 3).

4. Place hand so centerline of arm intersects center of bow.

5. Face of bow turns to right or left during draw.

5. Center hand behind bow, relax fingers.

6. Arrows group left of bull's-eye.

6. Relax bow hand so bow is not gripped. Use a bow sling. Make sure bow hand is not too far right on bow handle.

ERROR 🚫	CORRECTION
7. Arrows group right of bull's-eye.	7. Make sure bow hand is not too far left on bow handle.
8. Arrows group high on target.	8. Avoid pushing on bow with heel of bow hand at release.
9. When using straight wrist, wrist suddenly loses rigidity.	9. Let shot down; start over, maintaining straight wrist. If error occurs after shooting for period of time and you have difficulty correcting it, consider using low wrist.

Bow Hand Drills and Aids

1. Choosing a Bow Hand Position

Shoot 2 ends of 6 arrows each from 20 yards with a high wrist. Now do the same with a straight wrist, and finally with a low wrist. Changing your bow hand position is likely to move the impact point of your arrows from the bull's-eye. Do not be concerned with the locations of your groups right now, but note below by ''good'' or ''poor'' how *tight* each group was and how comfortable the position was. The position that produces the tightest groups and is the most comfortable one for you is the one you should try shooting with.

Success Goal = to determine the bow hand position that is the most comfortable and produces the tightest groups

Your Results =

High Wrist
    End 1: Comfort _____ Group _____
    End 2: Comfort _____ Group _____

Straight Wrist
    End 1: Comfort _____ Group _____
    End 2: Comfort _____ Group _____

Low Wrist
    End 1: Comfort _____ Group _____
    End 2: Comfort _____ Group _____

Position Chosen: _____

2. Tension Demonstration

In this drill you shoot 6-arrow ends at a target from 20 yards. Shoot 2 ends with the fingers of your bow hand rigidly extended and tense. Note your score and directional error. Now do the same for 2 more ends, purposely gripping the bow handle tightly with your bow hand. Finally, shoot 2 ends with a relaxed hold. Note which type of bow hand grip gives you the best results.

Success Goal = to demonstrate the benefits of a relaxed bow hand

Your Results =

Extended Fingers:
   End 1: Score _____ Error _____

   End 2: Score _____ Error _____

Tight Grip:
   End 1: Score _____ Error _____

   End 2: Score _____ Error _____

Relaxed Hold:
   End 1: Score _____ Error _____

   End 2: Score _____ Error _____

Best Grip: _____

Note

If a grip other than the relaxed one gave you better results, you may not be relaxing your bow hand enough. Practice the Relaxation Check (Drill 6) below.

3. Torque Check

Without an arrow take your stance and bow grip as usual, while an observer watches from a few feet downrange. As you draw the string back, the observer should note whether the back of the bow always faces the target or turns to the right or left. The observer can also watch a stabilizer or extended sight if you have these on your bow to see whether they point right or left during the draw. If the bow turns right or left, change your hand position on the handle until you can draw without torquing the bow.

Success Goal = 5 successive draws without torquing the bow

Your Score = (#) _____ draws

4. Consistency Check

Obtain two small pieces of tape or two dot stickers. Place one on the middle of the bow handle just above where you place your hand. Take your bow hand position and place the second sticker on your hand right below the other dot on the bow. Shoot 2 ends. Take your bow hand position, but before drawing, check to see whether the stickers or pieces of tape are aligned.

Success Goal = 10 of 12 shots in alignment

Your Score = (#) _____ shots aligned

5. Distance Practice

Bow hand errors become more obvious as you increase your distance from the target. Shoot 3 ends of 6 arrows at 20 yards, then 3 ends at 30 yards, and 3 ends at 40 yards. For each distance, plot your arrows on the targets at the right. Note your directional errors. Also, note whether the amount of error increased as the distance increased by indicating "same" or "more." Check items 6, 7, and 8 on the errors and corrections lists. Note whether your directional errors could be related to a flaw in bow hand technique.

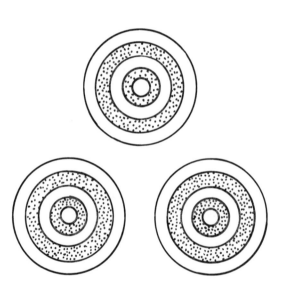

Success Goal = accurate ends despite increasing shooting distance

Your Results =

20 yards: Direction _____ Amount _____

30 yards: Direction _____ Amount _____

40 yards: Direction _____ Amount _____

Possible flaw in bow hand position: _____

_____

Note

If you used a high or straight wrist for this drill and found that you could not maintain your bow hand position as you shot more and more arrows, consider using a low-wrist position.

6. Relaxation Check

Extend your bow arm. Relax your wrist; if it is relaxed, it should droop toward the ground. Take your draw hand and hook the skin web between the thumb and forefinger of your bow hand. This mimics the pressure of the bow when it is drawn. Hold for a count of 3, trying to maintain a relaxed wrist and hand. When you let go with your draw hand, your bow hand should fall into its original drooping position. If it remains up, you have let tension develop in your wrist. Repeat 12 times.

Success Goal = 10 of 12 repetitions with a relaxed wrist

Your Score = (#) _____ repetitions with a relaxed wrist

Bow Hand Position
Keys to Success Checklist

If you are learning a new bow hand position, have a trained observer check you on the following points. Even after the new position becomes habit, it is easy to fall into the bad habit of tensing the bow wrist, hand, and fingers. Spotting a flaw early helps your shooting accuracy. It is often valuable to conduct the observation after you have been shooting continuously for a while and are more likely to be tired.

**Low-Wrist
Position**

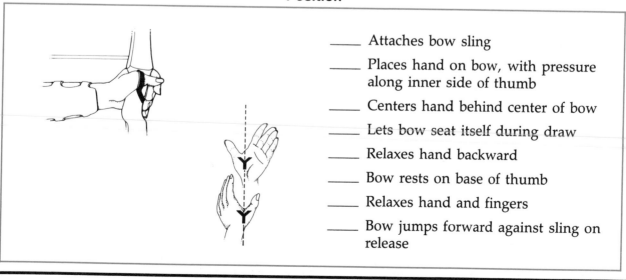

_____ Attaches bow sling

_____ Places hand on bow, with pressure along inner side of thumb

_____ Centers hand behind center of bow

_____ Lets bow seat itself during draw

_____ Relaxes hand backward

_____ Bow rests on base of thumb

_____ Relaxes hand and fingers

_____ Bow jumps forward against sling on release

High-Wrist Position

____ Attaches bow sling

____ Centers hand behind center of bow

____ Cocks wrist up; hand down

____ Maintains high wrist

____ Bow rests in skin web

____ Relaxes hand and fingers

____ Bow jumps forward against sling on release

Straight-Wrist Position

____ Attaches bow sling

____ Centers hand behind center of bow

____ Maintains straight wrist

____ Bow rests against skin web

____ Relaxes hand and fingers

____ Bow jumps forward against sling on release

Step 11   Selecting an Anchor Position

The anchor position you have been using is termed the *under-chin* anchor. There are two other anchor positions, the side anchor and the behind-the-neck anchor, and one of them may be better for you. This step gives you an opportunity to try different anchor positions. Once you decide which anchor position to use, your goal is to reproduce it as precisely as possible on every shot.

WHY VARY THE ANCHOR POINT?

The under-chin anchor used thus far is a common one, but it may not be the one best suited for your body structure or the type and style of archery you prefer. For example, it is sometimes difficult for archers with large hands or short necks to use the under-chin anchor. Time is also needed to anchor under the chin, and this is a disadvantage in bowhunting. The under-chin anchor tips the head slightly; some archers prefer to maintain a more natural head position.

To offset these disadvantages, many archers choose to use a *side* anchor. A third option is the *behind-the-neck* anchor, in which the draw hand thumb anchors behind the neck. This anchor takes longer to assume than the side anchor, so it is typically used only by target archers. However, it is a firm anchor that minimizes creeping.

Consider which form of archery you like best; being mindful of your body structure, you may want to try an anchor position other than the under-chin anchor you are using now. If you decide to stay with the under-chin anchor, take this opportunity to perfect it.

HOW TO USE THE VARIOUS ANCHOR POSITIONS

The Keys to Success in Figure 11.1 can guide you in trying a new anchor position. They also add more detail on the under-chin anchor than previous steps, should you decide to continue using and perfect that position. Once you decide which anchor to use, work to perfect it. The anchor position functions as a rear sight. A consistent anchor contributes much to accurate shooting, whereas a variable anchor points the arrow in various directions from shot to shot.

The side anchor can be used in a high or low position, depending on the accessories used. If you are not using a peep sight or kisser button, anchor to the side by placing the tip of your index finger in the corner of your mouth. If you are using a kisser button, place the kisser button between your lips in the corner of your mouth. Your draw hand is lower, with the index finger anchored under your jawbone. Your nose can be placed on the string for an extra reference point, even if a kisser button is used.

You can use the low side anchor without a kisser button by letting the string cross the corner of your mouth. Care must be taken to reproduce this anchor as precisely as possible from shot to shot. The peep sight, if used, is always aligned so that the bull's-eye and sight are seen in the center of the peep sight's opening.

With any anchor, the draw should be straight back—not out, and then in. The position should be identical from shot to shot. Your hand should be relaxed throughout the shot. Follow-through is always back over the rear shoulder, due to tension in the back.

Figure 11.1   Keys to Success: **Anchor Position**

**Under-Chin
Anchor**

1. Bring draw elbow back
2. Draw close to bow arm
3. Draw hand under chin
4. Touch string to chin and nose
5. Hand under jaw
6. Touch kisser button between lips
7. Align peep sight, if used
8. Relax back of hand
9. Keep wrist straight

Advantages

- Two-point contact on chin and nose is consistent
- Prevents overdrawing
- Low position on face allows you to shoot long distances with less extreme sight movement, especially with light-weight bow

Disadvantages

- Uncomfortable for archer with large hands or short neck
- Takes time to position
- Tips head

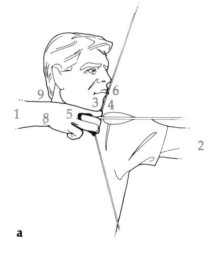

a

Side Anchor

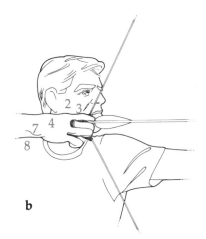

b

1. Bring draw elbow back
2. Draw straight back to side of face
3. Touch kisser button to corner of mouth
   or
   Touch forefinger to corner of mouth
4. Slide thumb under jaw
5. Put nose on string (low anchor)
6. Align peep sight, if used
7. Relax back of hand
8. Keep wrist straight

Advantages

- Quickly established
- Allows sighting down arrow shaft when shooting barebow
- Comfortable

Disadvantages

- Permits overdrawing
- Permits creeping

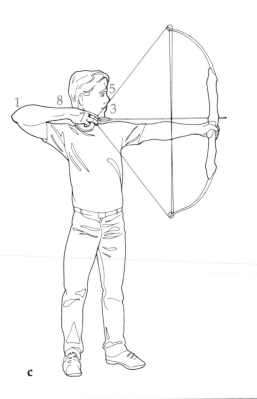

c

Behind-the-Neck Anchor

1. Bring draw elbow back
2. Draw close to bow arm
3. Feel string on nose and side of chin
4. Touch kisser button to corner of mouth
5. Place draw hand against neck
6. Place thumb behind neck, close to shoulder
7. Align peep sight, if used
8. Relax back of hand
9. Keep wrist straight

Advantages

- Minimizes creeping
- Firm and exact position
- Promotes good alignment in round-shouldered archer
- Permits longer draw length

Disadvantages

- Takes time to position
- Can feel awkward to position

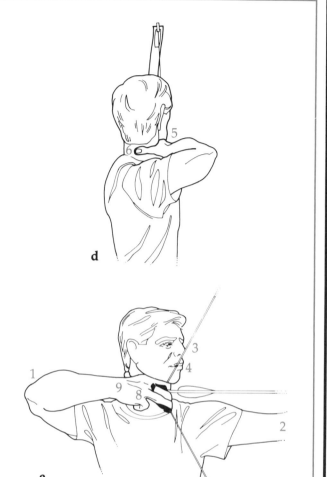

Anchoring and Release Errors

The anchor must be consistent from shot to shot. It must allow you to release the string cleanly, that is, so that it takes the straightest possible path forward. Achieving consistency and a clean release contributes to improved accuracy. Particularly if you are using a new anchor, evaluate your anchor and release to make them as perfect as possible. Have an experienced observer watch you or have someone take videotapes or photographs so that you can identify any errors in your anchor and release.

ERROR ⊘

CORRECTION

1. Draw hand comes away from head on release (plucks).

1. Make sure force for draw comes from back muscles and draw hand remains relaxed throughout. Check for indications that hand is tense, such as base knuckles or wrist being flexed; relax hand and wrist if you find them tense.

2. Draw hand fails to follow through (dead-releases).

2. Release string by relaxing hand, rather than forcing fingers open.

⊘

3. Three fingers come off string at slightly different times at release.

3. Release string by relaxing hand, rather than forcing fingers open; all three fingers should come off string at same time.

4. Kisser button contacts mouth in slightly different places from shot to shot.

4. Make sure that contact of draw hand with face or neck is consistent shot to shot. Feel for consistent contact with kisser button; if initial position is not correct, let down and restart shot. Make sure head is in same position shot to shot.

5. String crooked (torqued) because of the way draw hand is oriented at full draw.

5. Make sure back of draw hand is perpendicular to ground, not rotated palm-down.

6. Only tip of chin touches draw hand in under-chin anchor.

6. Slide draw hand up after reaching full draw to touch top of hand to chin and jawbone.

7. Forefinger and knuckle of draw hand contact side of chin and jaw in under-chin anchor.

7. Tuck hand underneath jawbone by drawing under chin and raising draw hand to touch chin.

ERROR 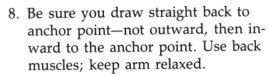 **CORRECTION**

8. Tension is felt in biceps or forearm.

8. Be sure you draw straight back to anchor point—not outward, then inward to the anchor point. Use back muscles; keep arm relaxed.

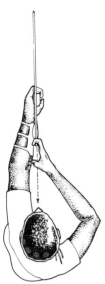

Anchoring Drills

1. Mirror Check

Take only your bow and stand at an angle toward a full-length mirror. Assume your stance; establish your bow hand hold and draw hook. Raise the bow and draw to an under-chin anchor. Check to see that your anchor position is correct. Repeat this with a side anchor and a behind-the-neck anchor.

Variation: Have a partner check your anchor.

Success Goal = 10 successive draws with each anchor position

Your Score =

(#) _____ draws, under-chin anchor

(#) _____ draws, side anchor

(#) _____ draws, behind-the-neck anchor

2. *Mimic With Eyes Closed*

Take only your bow and assume your stance, bow hand hold, and hook. Raise the bow and draw to an under-chin anchor with your eyes closed. Feel for the proper position; hold for a count of 3, maintaining relaxed hands; then ease the string back. This drill establishes your feel for proper anchor position. Repeat with a side anchor and a behind-the-neck anchor.

Success Goal = 10 successive repetitions with each anchor position

Your Score =

    (#) _____ repetitions, under-chin anchor

    (#) _____ repetitions, side anchor

    (#) _____ repetitions, behind-the-neck anchor

3. *Setting the Kisser Button*

In Drills 1 and 2 you tried the various anchor positions. Decide which one you will use for the near future. You can now install a kisser button (see Step 6) for this anchor position. Slip the kisser button onto the string above the nock locator. Now take a normal stance and draw to your anchor. Note whether you feel the kisser button above or below your lips. Let down and adjust the kisser button in the direction of your lips. Repeat this until the button is between your lips. Mark this location on the bowstring. If you are using personal equipment, attach the button to the string with an open ring that you clamp down with nocking pliers.

Variation: Have a partner move the button to the proper location while you hold at full draw.

Success Goal = to correctly position the kisser button

Your Results = height of kisser button above nock locator: _____

4. *Guided Blind Shoot*

Stand 7 yards from the target with a partner behind you. Assume your stance, nock an arrow, and establish your bow hand hold and your draw hook. Raise the bow. Then, with eyes closed, draw to the anchor you have chosen to use. Your partner should check the height of your bow arm to ensure a hit on the target, then say "okay." When you are ready, release. This drill establishes your feel for both the anchor and release without the visual distraction of aiming.

Success Goal = 10 repetitions with a clean release

Your Score = (#) _____ repetitions

5. Sight-Setting Drill

If you are now using a new anchor position, you need to reestablish your sight settings. Also, if you have made a slight change in your under-chin anchor, you need to check your sight settings.

Start at 10 yards. Shoot and adjust until you obtain an accurate sight setting. Move back to 15 yards, then 20, 25, 30, 35, and 40 yards, shooting until you have an accurate sight setting. If you are using a new anchor, there likely is more difference in your setting at a longer distance than a shorter.

Success Goal = to obtain an accurate sight setting at each distance

Your Results =

Sight settings: _____ 10 yards

_____ 15 yards

_____ 20 yards

_____ 25 yards

_____ 30 yards

_____ 35 yards

_____ 40 yards

6. Arrow Pattern Check

From 20 yards, shoot 2 ends of 6 arrows each. Plot your arrow patterns on targets a and b below. If you find directional errors consult the "Arrow Pattern Analysis" section in Step 8 (pp. 69-81). Focus particularly on any causes that are related to the anchor position or release. Try to correct these as you shoot 2 additional ends, plotting your arrow patterns on targets c and d.

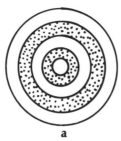 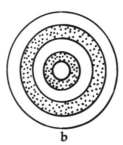 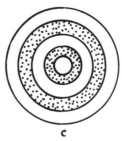 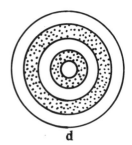

a   b   c   d

Success Goal = 2 final ends without directional error

Your Directional Errors =

a. _____ o'clock

b. _____ o'clock

c. _____ o'clock

d. _____ o'clock

7. Video Check

Have a partner or instructor videotape 12 of your shots in a row, focusing closely on your anchor and release. View the videotape once to check for proper mechanics of your release. Consult the error correction chart. View the tape again to check for shot-to-shot consistency.

Success Goal = 12 shots with consistent anchors

Your Score = (#) _____ shots with consistent anchors

8. Scoring Drill

Now that you have had a chance to perfect one of the anchor positions, check your success in scoring well. Start at 40 yards with an 80-centimeter target face; shoot 4 ends of 6 arrows each. Repeat this at 30, 20, and 10 yards.

Success Goal = to improve your score as you move closer

Your Score =

    40 yards, End 1 _____ points

                 End 2 _____ points

                 End 3 _____ points

                 End 4 _____ points

                 Total _____ points

    30 yards, End 1 _____ points

                 End 2 _____ points

                 End 3 _____ points

                 End 4 _____ points

                 Total _____ points

    20 yards, End 1 _____ points

                 End 2 _____ points

                 End 3 _____ points

                 End 4 _____ points

                 Total _____ points

    10 yards, End 1 _____ points

                 End 2 _____ points

                 End 3 _____ points

                 End 4 _____ points

                 Total _____ points

Anchor Position
Keys to Success Checklist

Because your anchor position functions as a rear sight, arrows are pointed differently from shot to shot if the anchor varies even slightly. This is true even if a bowsight is used. Have someone check you frequently to assure a correct and consistent anchor, using the keys appropriate for the anchor position you selected. They should check every key they observe in your performance.

Under-Chin Anchor

____ Initiates draw by moving draw elbow back, close to bow arm, straight back to anchor

____ Touches string to nose and chin

____ Slides draw arm unit up to touch edge of forefinger and hand to chin and jawbone

____ Places kisser button between lips

____ Relaxes draw hand; keeps wrist straight

Side Anchor

____ Initiates draw by moving draw elbow straight back to anchor

____ Places kisser button or tip of forefinger in corner of mouth

____ Touches string to nose if using kisser button

____ Positions thumb under jawbone

____ Relaxes draw hand; keeps wrist straight

Behind-the-Neck
Anchor

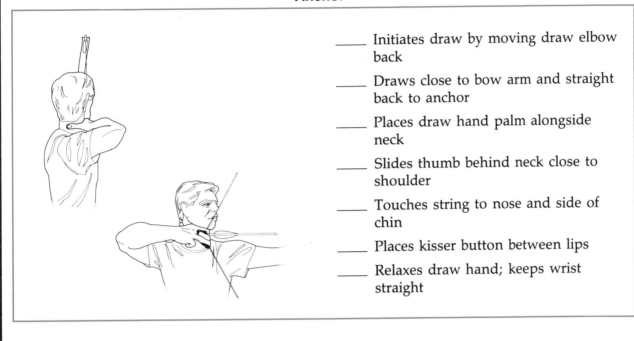

_____ Initiates draw by moving draw elbow back

_____ Draws close to bow arm and straight back to anchor

_____ Places draw hand palm alongside neck

_____ Slides thumb behind neck close to shoulder

_____ Touches string to nose and side of chin

_____ Places kisser button between lips

_____ Relaxes draw hand; keeps wrist straight

Step 12 Developing a Personal Mental Checklist

You explored ways to vary basic shooting form in the last three steps. If you chose to use any of the variations, your form checklist obviously is different than the one used in refining basic form. A mental checklist for shot preparation is highly personalized. You can use various stance, bow hand, and anchor positions, for example. Your checklist, therefore, reflects your unique style.

You will undoubtedly find yourself falling into bad habits from time to time. You should thus make specific checklist reminders regarding these aspects of your shooting until you again make the proper setup a habit. With these points in mind, you now take the step of developing a personal mental checklist for your shooting style.

WHY CREATE A MENTAL CHECKLIST?

Success in archery is related to shot-to-shot consistency. The more precisely you set up a shot and then replicate this setup, the tighter your arrows group. Archery is usually shot without the pressure of time. Therefore, you have ample time to make sure each shot is prepared correctly.

A mental checklist is a helpful way to proceed through shot setup. It reminds you to attend to the necessary aspects of shot preparation. If you tend to repeat the same form error, a checklist can include a specific reminder to avoid the error. Hence, a mental checklist helps you methodically and precisely prepare every shot in the same way.

Your checklist points can vary on a daily basis with shooting conditions. For example, an archer shooting at a target on a sloping hillside often unwittingly cants the bow. The addition of a mental checklist reminder to level the bow helps the archer check for a level bow on each and every shot.

HOW TO DEVELOP A PERSONAL CHECKLIST

Begin the development of your personal checklist by identifying the Keys to Success pertinent to your shooting style. A skeleton list of the Keys to Success appears in Figure 12.1. Where you might have decided to use a variation deviating from the Improving Shooting Accuracy Keys in Figure 5.1, a blank is left for you to fill in an appropriate cue. The Keys to Success in Figures 9.1, 10.1, and 11.1 can also help you come up with the pertinent cue.

With practice, you can streamline your checklist. The skeleton list below assumes that some of the simplest aspects of shooting are now habitual and need not be specified. Feel free to add anything you tend to overlook or do incorrectly.

Figure 12.1 Keys to Success: *Mental Checklist*

**Stance
Phase**

a

1. Assume stance: _____

b

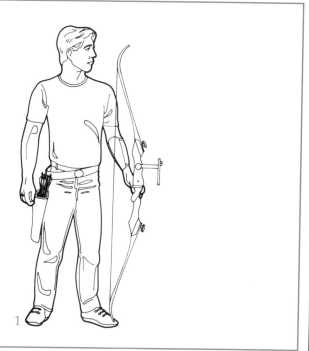

2. Nock arrow

**Draw and Aim
Phase**

c

1. Set bow hand: _____
2. Set draw hand hook

d

3. Raise bow, draw
4. Anchor: _____

e

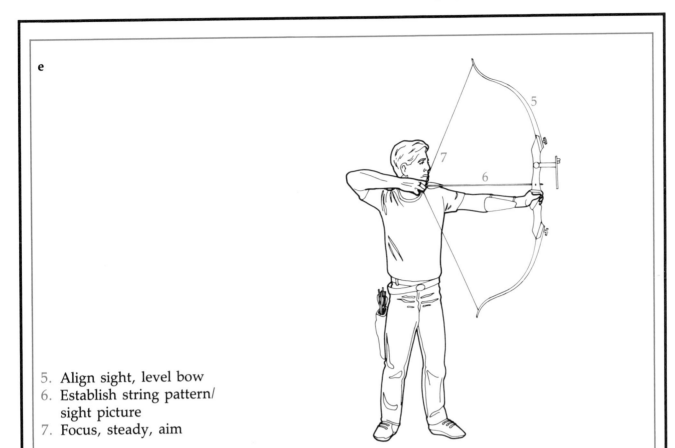

5. Align sight, level bow
6. Establish string pattern/
   sight picture
7. Focus, steady, aim

Release and
Follow-Through Phase

f

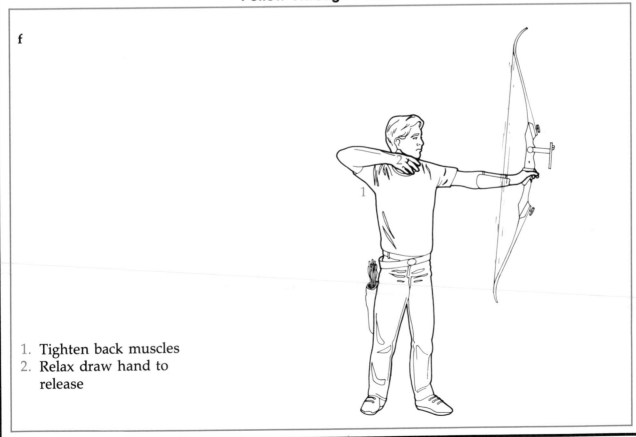

1. Tighten back muscles
2. Relax draw hand to
   release

g

3. Keep bow arm up and
   steady

Checklist and Practice Drills

1. Learning Your Checklist

Copy the Keys to Success that you have
chosen for your personal checklist onto a long,
narrow sheet of paper that you can attach to
the face of your upper or lower bow limb. As
an alternative, copy it with large lettering onto

a large index card and lay the card on the ground in front of you (anchor it on a windy day when shooting outdoors). Use your written checklist for your next two practice sessions.

Then see whether you can recite your checklist to a friend without reading it. When you can do so, shoot without the written list but remember to mentally go through your checklist on every shot.

Success Goal = to be able to recite your checklist perfectly

Your Score = (#) _____ attempts before reciting your checklist perfectly

2. Rehearsing-Aloud Drill

Shoot 4 ends at 20 yards. On each arrow, recall the items in your checklist aloud as you perform them up until you anchor. This reminds you to attend to each item. You have to go through the items during the anchor and aiming silently. After release, recall aloud your cues for maintaining follow-through.

Success Goal = to execute each item in your checklist just as you listed it while shooting 4 ends

Your Score = (#) _____ arrows shot with each step executed

3. Balloon Practice

At this point in learning to shoot well, you need continued practice. It is fun to break the monotony of practicing on the same target face. Blow up three balloons and tape them somewhere on the target face.

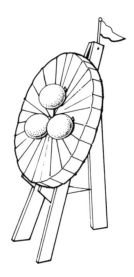

Try to pop all three balloons in 1 end from a distance of 20 yards. If you don't get all three balloons in 1 end, continue shooting until you have popped them all. Repeat this at 25 yards, then at 30 yards. Remember to use your personal checklist.

Success Goal = to pop the three balloons in 1 end at 20 and 25 yards, and in 2 ends at 30 yards

Your Score =

(#) _____ ends required at 20 yards

(#) _____ ends required at 25 yards

(#) _____ ends required at 30 yards

4. Tic-Tac-Toe

With a partner, obtain a 2 × 2-foot piece of paper or posterboard. Draw a tic-tac-toe pattern on the paper. Flip a coin to see who shoots first. You may select any shooting distance you like. Play tic-tac-toe, taking turns shooting, each shot counting if the arrow lands inside a box and does not touch any of the lines. However, you must recite your checklist during each shot as in Drill 2 above. If your partner catches you missing an item, you forfeit your turn. Repeat as time allows.

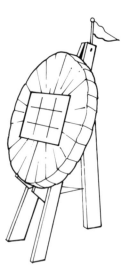

Success Goal = to win or draw at least half of the games played

Your Score = (#) _____ games won of _____ games played

5. *Subtract an Arrow*

Choose a partner. Mount an 80-centimeter face on the target butt. Shoot from a mutually agreed-upon distance. Each of you should wrap a piece of tape around 1 of your 6 arrows near the fletching to mark it.

Shoot your first 5 arrows, saving your marked arrow until last. After all 10 unmarked arrows have been shot, take turns shooting the marked arrows. You must each recite your personal checklist on this arrow. If your partner catches you leaving out an item (or vice versa), the arrow does not count in the score. If you execute your checklist successfully, the value of the marked arrow is subtracted from your partner's end score (it does not count toward your score). Repeat this 5 more times.

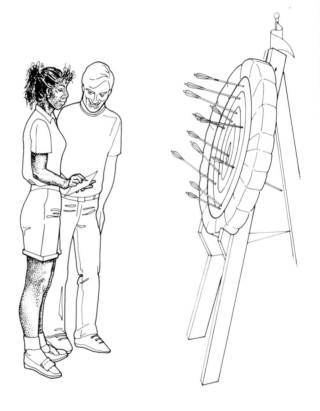

Success Goal = to win at least half of the ends

Your Score =

End 1: You _____ Partner _____

End 2: You _____ Partner _____

End 3: You _____ Partner _____

End 4: You _____ Partner _____

End 5: You _____ Partner _____

End 6: You _____ Partner _____

Wins: You _____ Partner _____

6. *Arrow Analysis*

Shoot 4 ends of 6 arrows each from a distance of 30 yards. Plot your arrows on the diagrams below. Identify any directional errors and use the ''Arrow Pattern Analysis'' lists in Step 8 to identify the possible causes of these directional errors. Now modify your personal mental checklist to include a reminder to correct the causes of these errors.

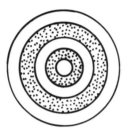 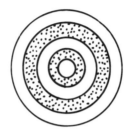 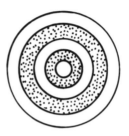 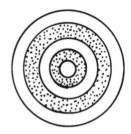

Success Goal = to update your mental checklist

Your Results =

Directional Errors: _____

Possible Causes: _____

_____

_____

Items Added to Checklist: _____

_____

_____

Mental
Keys to Success Checklist

Share your personal checklist below with your instructor or another trained observer. Have him or her check off the steps you remember to execute on a selected shot. If you miss one, be sure to emphasize it on subsequent shots.

Again, only a skeleton checklist is given below. You should fill in the unique elements of your shooting style for an observer, following Figure 12.1.

Stance
Phase

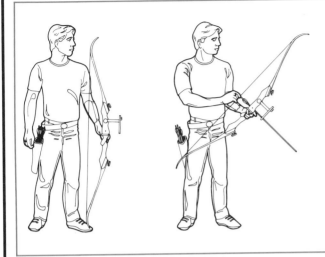

_____ Assumes stance: _____

_____

_____ Nocks arrow

Draw and Aim
Phase

_____ Sets bow hand: _____

_____

_____ Sets draw hand hook, hand relaxed

_____ Raises bow, draws

_____ Anchors: _____

_____

_____ Aligns sight, levels bow (Reports to observer after shot)

_____ Establishes string pattern and/or sight picture (Reports to observer after shot)

_____ Focuses on bull's-eye, steadies sight, aims (Reports to observer after shot)

Release and Follow-Through
Phase

_____ Tightens back muscles

_____ Relaxes draw hand to release

_____ Keeps bow arm up, head steady

_____ Reviews shot

Step 13   Scoring in Archery

Having practiced your basic and refined form, now you may enjoy shooting for score in the same format used for target archery tournaments. The first step toward participating in a tournament, in fact, is to learn the scoring procedures used. In this step you learn the rules for scoring arrows and have an opportunity to practice scoring.

WHY IS SCORING IMPORTANT?

In archery you can compare your performance against your own previous performance or the performance of other archers. In either case, the arrows shot must be scored consistently. Otherwise, you would obtain very different scores if, for example, one time you gave arrows cutting two rings the higher value and another time you gave them the lower value.

It is also important that all scores be recorded the same way, particularly in a tournament with many people shooting. Questions may arise regarding the accuracy of a score at the conclusion of shooting, and the scorecard is the official and permanent record of what really happened. Also, some tournaments break ties by counting the number of hits on the target, the number of bull's-eyes, and so on. All archers must be aware of scoring procedures and must keep score accurately in order to compare their performances.

HOW TO SCORE

Each governing body and tournament can have specific rules for scoring, but the guidelines below are common to most sets of rules.

1. The traditional target face in archery consists of five concentric scoring zones—gold/yellow, red, blue, black, and white, from the center outward. Each color zone is divided into two equal-sized zones by a thin line. This results in 10 scoring zones of equal width. The innermost zone has a value of 10, the next 9, and so on through the outermost zone, with a value of 1. The target face can be of various diameters, but the scoring zones must all be of equal width.

2. The lines dividing the scoring zones are considered to be entirely within the higher scoring area. Any arrow touching a dividing line, even slightly, is therefore assigned the higher value.

3. Arrows are scored by the position of the shafts in the face at the time arrows are scored. Arrows sometimes enter the target at an angle or vibrate on impact, tearing into an adjacent scoring ring. These tears are ignored and the arrows are scored as they are sitting in the target face.

4. You are not allowed to touch any of the arrows in the target or the target face itself until all the arrows are scored and any questionable scores are decided upon by the appropriate official (see Figure 13.1).

Figure 13.1   An official ''calling'' an arrow.

5. Arrows that skip into the target after striking the ground receive a score of 0.

6. If an arrow passes through the target face but not the target butt, it can be pushed back through the butt and target face to determine which scoring zone it penetrated.

7. If an arrow passes completely through the target butt or bounces out of the scoring area, and is witnessed by another archer or tournament official, it is scored as 7 points unless the procedure in the tournament is to mark the target face at the impact point of each arrow during scoring. In this case, the pass-through or bounce-out arrow is scored by the hole made in the target face.

8. If you shoot more arrows than the number specified to comprise an end in the round being shot, only the lowest scoring arrows in the number comprising an end are scored. For example, if an end consists of 6 arrows and you shoot 7, only the lowest scoring 6 arrows are scored.

9. If you do not shoot all the arrows allowed in an end and do not discover this before the signal to score or retire from the shooting line, those arrows are lost from scoring.

10. Any arrows you shoot into a target other than the particular target assigned to you are not scored.

11. An arrow that embeds itself in another arrow and, hence, does not reach the target face is scored as the same value as the arrow in which it is embedded.

When shooting in a tournament, each archer is assigned to a target at check-in. Scorecards are either given to the archer or placed at the assigned target. Typically, four archers are assigned to a target (see Figure 13.2). These archers perform specific scoring duties, either by assignment of the tournament officials or by mutual agreement of the archers. One archer serves as target captain and calls out the value of each arrow on the target, archer by archer. If any of the other archers disagree

Figure 13.2 The archers assigned to a target share scoring duties.

with a call, a tournament official is called to make the final decision on that arrow. Two of the remaining archers keep score on independent sets of scorecards. They may cross-check each archer's end score and running score on each end so that discrepancies can be quickly rectified. The fourth archer retrieves any arrows that miss the target and may assist the target captain by checking the scores announced.

The tournament officials usually provide scorecards that are prepared specifically for the round being shot. Examples are given in Figure 13.3a and b. The value of each arrow is entered on the card in the appropriate area, as are the end score and, often, a running score. Although the two archers keeping score on each target must cross-check the scores, the archer being scored is responsible for seeing that everything on the card, including addition of the score, is in proper order before the scorecard is turned in at the conclusion of the day's shooting. In some tournaments an archer can be disqualified for scorecard errors. When the archer is satisfied that the scorecard is correct, each scorekeeper and the archer sign the card before it is submitted (see Figure 13.4).

FITA

Name							
City							

Meters						Hits	Score
					Total		

Meters						Hits	Score
					Total		

50 Meters	Hits	Score	30 Meters	Hits	Score
Total			Total		

	Hits	Score
Meters		
Meters		
50 Meters		
30 Meters		
Total Score		

NAA 900

Name	Example						
Class	MW 1:00			Total Score			
Date	February 3					Hits	Score
9	9	7	6	6	3	6	40
10	8	7	7	5	—	5	37
8	8	7	7	4	4	6	38
10	7	6	6	3	—	5	32
8	7	6	5	5	5	6	36
30 Yard Total						28	183
_____ Yard Total							
_____ Yard Total							

Figure 13.3a Scorecards prepared for a FITA round, left, and an NAA 900 round, right. The scorecard on the right is partially completed. The highest scoring arrows are recorded first.

Scholastic Round

Name		
Class		

40 Yards		Hits	Score
Distance Score			

30 Yards			
Distance Score			
Total Score			

Columbia Round

Name		
Class		

50 Yards		Hits	Score
Distance Score			

40 Yards			
Distance Score			

30 Yards			
Distance Score			
Total Score			

Junior American Round

Name		
Class		

50 Yards		Hits	Score
Distance Score			

40 Yards			
Distance Score			

30 Yards			
Distance Score			
Total Score			

Figure 13.3b Scorecards prepared for various competitive rounds.

Archery   *   Games of the XXIII Olympiad   *   Men

1	19A PACE	USA 1930	6	9A VERVINCK	BEL 1859	ARROW SHOT 216
2	11A MCKINNEY	USA 1895	7	20A GO BIERENDAL	SWE 1856	NEW RECORD 653
3	8C YAMAMOTO	JPN 1895	8	158 RUKIMIN	INA 1842	OLYMPIC RECORD 70M
4	9C MATSUSHITA	JPN 1877	9	10A DE KONING	BEL 1840	DOUBLE FITA 634
5	28 POIKOLAINEN	FIN 1876	10	7A MEYERS	USA 1836	THIS ROUND 653

* * * * *   Long Beach, California   * * * * *

☆ ☆ ☆ ☆ ☆ ☆ ☆ ☆

Figure 13.4 The scoreboard at the end of two days of competition in men's archery at the XXIII Olympiad in California.

Scoring Drills

1. Scoring by End

At the right are four targets with the location of shot arrows marked by Xs. In the blank scorecard place the value of each arrow in the appropriate space, with the arrows of greater value to the left. You should also indicate the number of *hits*, or arrows striking the target face, as well as the total score for the end and the running score as additional ends are shot. Double-check your score by adding the column of end scores and comparing the result with the running score.

End 1: One arrow missed the target.

End 2: One arrow bounced out of the target, which was witnessed by another archer.

End 3: One arrow skipped into the 2 ring after striking the ground, and another is embedded in the arrow in the 9 ring.

End 4: Seven arrows are in the target face.

Success Goal = correctly scoring all 4 ends

Your Score =

E n d	Scorecard					Hits	End Score	Running Score
1								
2								
3								
4								

Total: _____ _____

Check your results against the following answer key:

End	Scorecard						Hits	End Score	Running Score
1	10	7	5	4	3	0	5	29	29
2	9	7	6	5	4	1	6	32	61
3	9	9	6	6	5	0	5	35	96
4	8	8	8	6	6	6	6	42	138

Total: 22   138

Step 14 Tournament Shooting

It is helpful to periodically put repetitious practice aside and submit your skills to the test. This provides a motivating landmark for which you can prepare, bringing your mental and physical skills together. The results also motivate you to continue practicing and striving for new goals. This step familiarizes you with archery tournaments and gives you an opportunity to shoot a tournament score, either alone or with a group of archers.

WHY PARTICIPATE IN A TOURNAMENT?

Throughout learning a skill such as archery, you undoubtedly find it helpful to have clear goals. This is particularly true once you have learned the basics and need continued practice and refinement to reach a higher level. Shooting for a score provides a basis for setting goals by score; you can set your sights on obtaining an appropriately higher score the next time you score.

Monitoring your scores over time tells you how you are progressing; scoring is a source of feedback on your archery skill progress. If you improve upon your previous scores, it is likely that your form is good and you are on the right track. A drop in score can signal that you have unknowingly fallen into a bad habit. You can then review your form for the basics and reestablish proper form.

Archery is the type of sport in which the competition is within yourself more than it is against another archer. Yet, scores also provide a means of comparing your skill with that of other archers.

HOW TO SHOOT IN A TOURNAMENT

Before the day of a tournament, you have several responsibilities. One is to see that all equipment is, first, in safe condition and, second, in condition to provide the best possible shooting efficiency. Inspect your arrows and straighten any if necessary. Prepare a backup bowstring. Inspect the nock locator and serving. Inspect the bowsight and tighten any screws. Inspect the arrow rest and cushion plunger or spring rest. In other words, you should take the time to see that all the equipment is prepared to perform as expected. Furthermore, if you are competing with a bowsight, you must obtain sight settings for all the distances that will be shot in the tournament.

Shooting in a tournament is controlled by a tournament official with the signals established earlier. One whistle blast typically indicates that archers on the shooting line can begin shooting. Two blasts signal that archers can cross the shooting line to score. Three or more blasts mean that shooting should cease immediately because an emergency situation exists.

Large tournaments often have multiple shooting lines. That is, half the archers assigned to a target step to the line to shoot their ends, then retire from the line while the remaining archers shoot—all before any arrows are scored (see Figure 14.1). In this case, another single whistle blast is used to indicate the end of shooting for one line and to call the second group to the line. Yet another single blast indicates that the second shooting line can begin shooting.

Tournament officials often establish a time limit for shooting the arrows within an end. The time limit chosen depends upon the number of arrows shot in each end, but it is also variable across tournaments. You should check to see whether a time limit will be in effect and, if so, how long it will be. Usually a warning signal is given when only 30 seconds remain in the time span.

If your equipment fails while you are on the shooting line, most tournament rules provide a time period during which you can repair or replace the equipment. If this should happen,

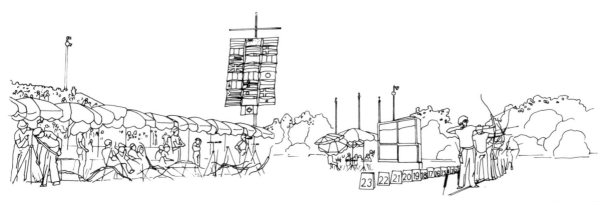

Figure 14.1 Half of the archers at this tournament shoot while the others await their turn from a position well behind the shooting line.

raise your bow while on the shooting line to signal the tournament official. You will be given an opportunity to shoot missed arrows at a later time, provided you can make the necessary repairs in the time allowed.

The exact number of arrows shot in a scoring round, the size of the target, and the shooting distances are variable. This variety often adds to the interest of target shooting. Each round provides its own challenge. Examples of the common scoring rounds are given in Table 14.1. Though these are the established archery rounds, archers are always free to design their own or modify an established round, provided all participants are made aware of the rules beforehand.

An archery tournament provides an oppor-

tunity to make new friends and renew old acquaintances. Between shooting ends, you can visit with other archers or friends, or keep to yourself, as you prefer. It is common courtesy, however, not to disturb archers who are on the line shooting, either directly or indirectly by talking loudly and so on. You should never talk while on the shooting line, unless it is necessary to the conduct of the tournament. It is also courteous not to distract fellow archers on either side by moving onto or off of the shooting line while they are at full draw. Among some it is traditional to remain on the shooting line until the archer on either side has finished shooting all arrows, so that no archer is left on the line alone to finish shooting.

Table 14.1 Popular Target Rounds

Round	Number of arrows per distance	Size of face	Number of arrows/end	Perfect score	Age group
FITA Men	36 at 90 m 36 at 70 m 36 at 50 m 36 at 30 m	122 cm 80 cm	6 (shot 3-3)	1440	Adult
FITA Women	36 at 70 m 36 at 60 m 36 at 50 m 36 at 30 m	122 cm 80 cm	6 (shot 3-3)	1440	Adult
Metric 900	30 at 60 m 30 at 50 m 30 at 40 m	122 cm	6 (shot 3-3)	900	Adult
Metric Easton 600	20 at 60 m 20 at 50 m 20 at 40 m	122 cm	5	600	Adult

Table 14.1 Popular Target Rounds (Cont.)

Round	Number of arrows per distance	Size of face	Number of arrows/end	Perfect score	Age group
Metric Collegiate 600	20 at 50 m 20 at 40 m 20 at 30 m	122 cm	5	600	Adult
American	30 at 60 yd 30 at 50 yd 30 at 40 yd	48 in. (scored 9-1)	6	810	Adult
Columbia	24 at 50 yd 24 at 40 yd 24 at 30 yd	48 in. (scored 9-1)	6	648	Adult
"720" Collegiate	24 at 50 m 24 at 40 m 24 at 30 m	80 cm	6	720	Adult
Junior Metric 900	30 at 50 m 30 at 40 m 30 at 30 m	122 cm	6	900	12-15 yr
Cadet Metric 900	30 at 40 m 30 at 30 m 30 at 20 m	122 cm	6	900	Under 12 yr
Interscholastic Metric	36 at 50 m 36 at 30 m	122 cm 80 cm	6	720	14-18 yr
Modified Collegiate, Boys	20 at 50 m 20 at 40 m 20 at 30 m	122 cm 80 cm	5	600	14-18 yr
Modified Collegiate, Girls	20 at 40 m 20 at 30 m 20 at 20 m	122 cm 80 cm	5	600	14-18 yr
Junior Metric	36 at 60 m 36 at 50 m 36 at 40 m 36 at 30 m	122 cm 80 cm	6 (shot 3-3)	1440	12-15 yr
Cadet Metric	36 at 45 m 36 at 35 m 36 at 25 m 36 at 15 m	122 cm 80 cm	6 (shot 3-3)	1440	Under 12 yr
Junior American	30 at 50 yd 30 at 40 yd 30 at 30 yd	48 in. (scored 9-1)	6	810	12-15 yr
Cadet American	30 at 40 yd 30 at 30 yd 30 at 20 yd	48 in. (scored 9-1)	6	810	Under 12 yr
Junior Columbia	24 at 40 yd 24 at 30 yd 24 at 20 yd	48 in. (scored 9-1)	6	648	Under 12 yr
FITA I Indoor	30 at 18 m	40 cm	3	300	Adult
FITA II Indoor	30 at 25 m	60 cm	3	300	Adult
Modified FITA Indoor	30 at 18 m	80 cm	3	300	14-18 yr
NAA 300 Indoor	60 at 20 yd	16 in. (scored 5-1)	5	300	Adult
Chicago Indoor	96 at 20 yd	16 in. (scored 9-1)	6	864	Adult

Practice Drills

1. Modified Metric 900 Round

Shoot a modification of the Metric 900 round, using the distances of 40, 30, and 20 meters rather than the official distances. Consult Table 14.1 to find the target face size and the number of arrows shot at each distance. You have the option of retrieving and scoring your arrows after shooting 6 arrows or after shooting 3 arrows.

You can shoot your score alone or with a group of archers. If you shoot with a group, decide who calls the arrow values on a target, who scores, and so on, as described in Step 13. You should also follow the scoring rules given in Step 13. One archer can also control the shooting line as described in this step. Record your score on the scorecard below.

Success Goal = to complete a modified Metric 900 round

Your Score =

Name								
Class								
			40 Meters				Hits	Score
Distance Score								
			30 Meters					
Distance Score								
			20 Meters					
Distance Score								
Total Score								

2. Interscholastic Metric Round

Shoot an Interscholastic Metric round from 40 and 30, rather than 50 and 30, meters. Note that you need two different sizes of target faces for this round (see Table 14.1). Follow the scoring rules given in Step 13. Again, you can shoot alone or with a group. Members of the group should act as target captain, scorer, and tournament officials, as mutually decided upon.

Success Goal = to complete a modified Interscholastic Metric round

Your Score =

Name							
Class							
			40 Meters			Hits	Score
		Distance Score					
			30 Meters				
		Distance Score					
		Total Score					

Step 15 Mental Approach to Archery

Performance in any sport goes beyond simply moving body parts in a certain way. There is always a mental side to performing well. In this step the mental aspects of archery are identified and you are given an opportunity to improve your mental approach to shooting.

WHY IS THE MENTAL APPROACH TO ARCHERY IMPORTANT?

From your experience with other sports and now with archery, you can see that the movements involved in archery are relatively simple. Most participants can develop good shooting form if they have an interest in doing so. What often distinguishes elite performers from good performers is their mental approach to archery, which includes concentration, relaxation, and confidence. You can enhance your performance by learning to control your mental approach to shooting (see Figure 15.1).

HOW TO DEVELOP CONCENTRATION

Throughout our earlier steps to success, we emphasized the necessity of repeating as exactly as possible every aspect of putting a shot together. This requires concentration. Letting your mind wander to other things and forgetting any critical aspect of shooting form makes for error.

In the previous step, you developed a personal mental checklist. Following the checklist in every detail on every shot maximizes the number of good shots you make. Of course, your checklist may need updating from time to time. Yet, your ability to concentrate on putting a shot together by moving through the list is related to your success. It is often said that the secret to archery is learning to make the perfect shot and then repeating it over and over again.

It is easy to say that concentration is the key to good shooting. What is difficult is knowing which aspects of putting a shot together need your attention. This is difficult in part because they change as you acquire greater archery skill. In the early steps, you may recall, the Keys to Success and Keys to Success Checklists included shot preparation details that were later dropped; with practice they had become second nature. As you acquire skill, you trim your checklists of items needing conscious attention to a minimum so you can devote more of your attention to aiming.

Ideally, on each and every shot, you should give your conscious attention to the items on your checklist up until you aim. Consider your stance, bow hand position, draw hand position, anchor, leveling, and so on. If everything feels right, feels it is as it should be, then aim. One hundred percent of your concentration must now be devoted to aiming. Your concentration should be so intense that it seems to burn a hole in the middle of the bull's-eye. Nothing should interfere with the aiming process.

The physical aspects of the release are turned over to your subconscious. You must trust that if there is any indication that the shot is not right, you can assume conscious control and let the shot down. Otherwise, your subconscious takes care of making the release happen at the right time. You do not have to worry about exactly when to make the release happen.

Champion athletes sometimes report that they feel as if they were in a trance as they compete. This feeling probably reflects intense concentration on their goals, such as aiming at the bull's-eye in archery, and turning the physical execution of their skills over to their subconscious.

HOW TO RELAX

Shooting is a rather strange mixture of tension and relaxation, compared to most sport skills. You must hold upward of 25 pounds of force while you hold the bow steady. At the same time, the very act of releasing is a relaxation of your draw hand, and you must maintain a completely relaxed bow hand throughout the shot, release, and follow-through.

You must learn to be selective regarding which parts of the body are under tension and which are relaxed. It is helpful to practice relaxing specific parts of your body, so that when you cue your bow hand and draw hand to relax at full draw, they do relax.

You may find it difficult to maintain relaxation under certain situations. Often when an archer really wants to shoot well, to really put an arrow in the bull's-eye, there is a tendency to tighten the hands so that the bowsight is kept on the bull's-eye. This is self-defeating because eventually a tight bow hand causes bow torque, and a tight draw hand works against a smooth release.

Should you decide to shoot archery competitively, expect the natural experience of nervousness. This comes with competition in most sports. Unlike most other sports, however, in archery you do not move about. You do not run, you do not hit a ball, you do not throw a ball; doing these could relieve some of the counterparts of nervousness. Instead, you must simply relax and hold steady! Accept the fact that you will be nervous, but give your attention to concentrating on each and every shot. Practice relaxing on cue so that you can relax even in a competitive situation.

HOW TO DEVELOP CONFIDENCE

For an arrow to hit the center of the bull's-eye, you must believe it will hit the center of the bull's-eye. You must have confidence that each and every one of the arrows shot has the potential to be a bull's-eye. Remember, success in archery competition comes not from shooting just one bull's-eye, but from scoring high when all of the arrows shot are totaled up. As you perfect your form and practice, you build confidence. You come to believe that you control each and every shot.

What undermines confidence, though? There are probably many causes. A common problem with archers is trying to please others with their shooting. That is, many archers want to live up to someone else's expectations, even on those days when, try as they might, nothing seems to work well. Yet, the only one you truly need to satisfy with your shooting is yourself. If you make a mistake, don't spend your time trying to explain it away to everyone around you. Accept it and go on.

It is easy in archery to blame the equipment for mistakes. However, if the equipment was working well last week or a few shots ago, and you have checked to see that it is in good working order, then the equipment is not to blame. It is important not to externalize shortcomings onto the equipment. All an externalizing archer really does is lose confidence in being able to shoot a bull's-eye.

When archers make a mistake, it is common to see them beginning to expect that mistake again. They talk about and think about making the mistake again; they undermine their confidence. If you find yourself verbalizing a negative statement about your shooting, either aloud or to yourself, stop. Turn it around to a positive statement. For example, if you find yourself saying, "Oh, no—it's windy, and the last time I shot in the wind I scored terribly," turn this statement around. Say, "The wind will give me a chance to improve over my last score on a windy day." You must expect that you will do well.

Some archers undermine their confidence when they set unrealistically high goals for themselves. For example, an archer who has been shooting 270 on a 300 round consistently for the last several weeks may go to a tournament wanting to shoot 280. If the 280 happens, great. However, is it realistic to expect to shoot above average in the tournament? Of course not! This archer is predestined to come back from the tournament disappointed and discouraged when anything but a 280 is shot. If the goal had instead been to shoot 270 and that is achieved, the archer is building—rather than undermining—confidence.

John Williams, the 1972 Olympic gold medalist, recommends setting your scoring goals conservatively. Even in practice, if you set what is really the minimum score you would ever want to shoot on a given round, your chances of feeling confident and positive after every practice session are good. Setting the minimum goal makes you work to achieve at least that level. Most often, you score above it, and in your mind you are then that many points "up," rather than points "down." When you set a very high goal and fail to reach it, you acquire a negative mind-set, even if your score was really a very good one.

Figure 15.1 **Keys to Success:** **Mental Approach**

Stance
Phase

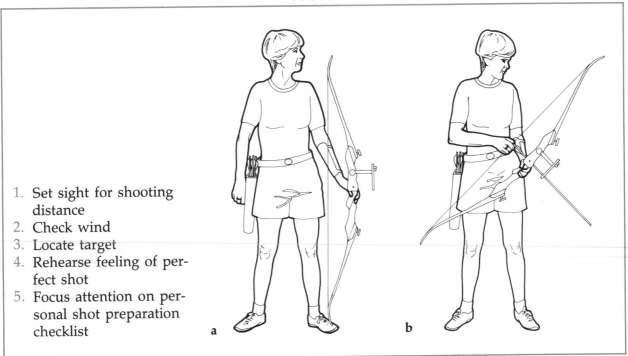

1. Set sight for shooting distance
2. Check wind
3. Locate target
4. Rehearse feeling of perfect shot
5. Focus attention on personal shot preparation checklist

a   b

Draw and Aim
Phase

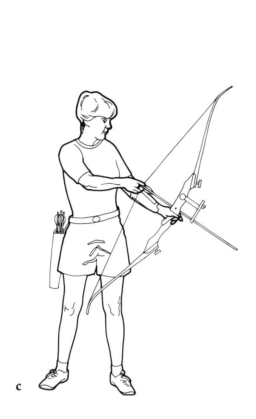

c

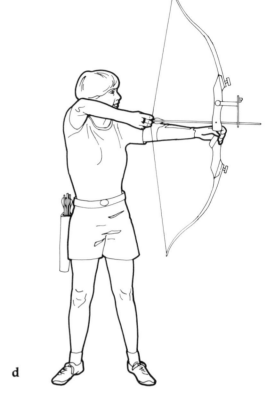

d

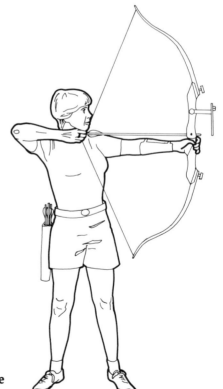

e

1. Continue through checklist
2. If setup feels right, cue "relax"
3. Shift attention to aiming
4. Aim at bull's-eye, repeating, "Aim, aim, aim"

Release and
Follow-Through Phase

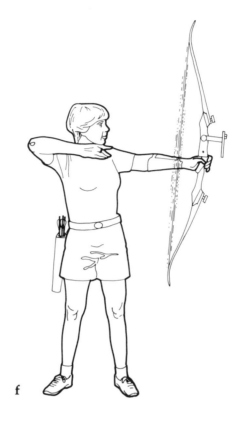

f

1. Release explosion occurs
2. Maintain concentration
   on bull's-eye through
   release

g

Detecting Mental Approach Errors

Often an archer does not realize that negative thoughts and overt statements are replacing a positive approach to success. The questions below encourage you to examine your thoughts and actions for evidence of a negative mind-set, then offer a suggestion for building a positive mind-set.

ERROR 🚫

CORRECTION

ERROR	CORRECTION
1. You verbalize negative statements about your shooting.	1. Stop statement immediately and formulate positive statement on same topic. Practice Thought Stopping Drill.
2. You hold a visual image of a bad shot and keep seeing it over and over.	2. Stop imagery of bad shot; mentally rehearse perfect shot that lands in middle of bull's-eye.
3. You consistently fail to meet goals.	3. You may be setting goals too high; consider your recent average, then set minimum goal slightly below this average.
4. You think about other things while you shoot.	4. Practice concentrating outside of archery sessions. While shooting focus your attention on preparing shot. Practice the Concentration Drills in this step.
5. You think about form while you should be aiming.	5. Shift attention completely to aiming. It may help to repeat a verbal cue over and over, such as "aim, aim, aim." Practice the Verbal Cue Drill (see Concentration Drill 3).

Concentration Drills

Just as you have repetitiously practiced your physical form, it is necessary to repetitiously practice a positive mental approach to archery. Simply saying "I'll have to concentrate today" may not be sufficient, particularly under the pressure of scoring. A positive mental approach must be practiced.

1. Concentration Exercise

You can practice your concentration outside archery practices with a concentration grid. This is a 10×10 grid filled with scrambled two-digit numbers from 00 through 99. In 1 minute, see how many consecutive numbers you can put a slash (/) through, starting with 11.

85	61	55	84	27	51	78	59	52	13
57	29	33	28	60	92	04	97	90	31
86	18	70	32	96	65	39	80	77	49
46	88	00	76	87	71	95	98	81	01
42	62	34	48	82	89	47	35	17	10
94	69	56	44	67	93	11	07	43	72
14	91	02	53	79	05	22	54	74	58
66	20	40	06	68	99	75	26	15	41
45	83	24	50	09	64	08	38	30	36
19	12	63	03	73	21	23	16	37	25

Success Goal = at least 25 slashed (i.e., from 11 through 35) in 1 minute

Your Score = (#) _____ slashed

2. Target Attention

Obtain a target face. Sit quietly, looking at the bull's-eye of the target. If distracting thoughts enter your mind, bring your attention back to the bull's-eye. You need not try to shut out thoughts—just bring your attention back to the bull's-eye.

Success Goal = to attend to a target for 4 minutes

Your Score = (#) _____ minutes attention

3. Verbal Cue Drill

Shoot 2 ends of 6 arrows each from any distance you choose. Consciously prepare each shot to the point of aiming. When you are ready to aim, say to yourself, "Aim, aim, aim," leaving the technical details to your subconscious, until the release occurs.

Success Goal = 12 repetitions with focus on the bull's-eye at release

Your Score = (#) _____ repetitions with the sight on the bull's-eye at release

Relaxation Drills

1. Hand and Arm Relaxation Drill

Practice this drill in a quiet place where you can sit or lie down comfortably. Go through the following:

a. Bend your right hand back. Hold for 10 seconds, then relax. Repeat.
b. Bend your right hand forward. Hold for 10 seconds, then relax. Repeat.
c. Repeat parts a and b with your left hand.
d. Repeat part a with half as much tension on your hold. Do the same with part b.
e. Repeat part d with your left hand.
f. Repeat part a with just enough tension that you feel the hold. Do the same with part b.
g. Repeat part f with your left hand.
h. Bend your right elbow. Hold for 10 seconds, then relax. Repeat. Repeat with your left elbow.
i. Repeat part h with half as much tension.
j. Repeat part h with barely enough tension to feel.
k. Clench your fist and tighten your whole right arm. Hold for 10 seconds, then relax. Repeat.
l. Repeat k with your left arm.

Success Goal = to work, for at least 9 minutes, through the relaxation list above to achieve a relaxed state

Your Results = (#) _____ minutes spent with this relaxation exercise

2. Visualization

Practice this exercise in a quiet place where you can sit or lie comfortably. You can play quiet music if you like. Close your eyes. Imagine you are lying on a warm, sunny beach. Try to imagine how the sand and sun feel. Then try to imagine the sound of the ocean. Add more and more detail to your mental picture.

Variation: Imagine being in any location or situation that you consider relaxing.

Success Goal = to achieve a more relaxed state than you were in previously

Your Results = (check one)

_____ more relaxed than before

_____ just as relaxed as before

_____ less relaxed than before

Confidence Drills

1. Mental Rehearsal

At a regular practice session, shoot as you normally do. After any shot you consider a mistake, mentally rehearse the feel of a good shot and see the arrow hitting the bull's-eye before taking your next shot.

Success Goal = to mentally rehearse 12 shots

Your Score = (#) _____ shots mentally rehearsed

2. Imagery Practice

Sit quietly with your eyes closed. Practice imaging by trying to see every detail of a close friend's face. Make the image as vivid as possible, almost as though you were seeing this friend on television. When you can do this well, image your bow, including every detail possible. Then image yourself performing with the bow. See every detail and hear the sounds that accompany shooting. Feel your muscles as they tense or relax. Note that you can image your performance either from the ''outside'' as if you were seeing yourself on television, or from the ''inside'' as it actually feels to perform.

Success Goal = to image for 4 minutes

Your Score = (#) _____ minutes imaging

3. Thought Stopping

Below you will find several examples of negative statements about archery performance. Write a positive counterpart to each. Speak these statements aloud. Then write several negative statements you find yourself saying and their positive counterparts. Speak the positive ones aloud several times.

Success Goal = to write 6 positive statements about archery performance

Your Change =   **Your Positive Statements**

a. From ''It is so windy I cannot keep the
   arrows on the target'' to

   _____

b. From ''I can't shoot well from 40
   yards'' to

   _____

c. From ''I'm afraid I'll miss the whole
   target'' to

   _____

Your additional negative statements:

d. _____

   _____ to

   _____

e. _____

   _____ to

   _____

f. _____

   _____ to

   _____

4. Goal-Setting Drill

Athletes often overlook setting goals for performance on several levels. For example, goals
can be set for the very near future or the distant future. Considering your recent archery performance, write goals for the time lines listed below. Also, give a target date for achieving your
longer-term goals.

Success Goal = to establish goals in 4 time frames

Your Goals =   **Target Date**

   a. Next practice: _____

      _____   _____

   b. Short-term: _____

      _____   _____

   c. Intermediate-term: _____

      _____   _____

   d. Long-term: _____

      _____   _____

Mental Approach
Keys to Success Checklist

The checklist below can give you a methodical way to check your own mental approach to shooting. After completing a shot, you will have to check those keys that you know you executed. An observer will not be able to check you on these points. Notice that your initial focus is on external conditions, such as the shooting distance and wind. Then your attention is shifted to internal factors, particularly your personal form checklist and aiming.

Stance
Phase

_____ Adjust sight for shooting distance

_____ Check wind conditions if outdoors

_____ Locate your target when target faces are close together

_____ Image yourself shooting a perfect shot

_____ Focus attention on preparing physical shot via form checklist

Draw and Aim
Phase

_____ Continue shot preparation through anchoring and leveling bow

_____ If setup feels right, use word "relax" to cue relaxation, especially in hands

_____ Shift attention to aiming, repeating word *aim* if necessary

Release and Follow-Through
Phase

_____ Release explosion occurs

_____ Maintain concentration on bull's-eye throughout release and follow-through

_____ Review shot, then image shooting perfect shot if you had made mistake

Step 16 Tuning Your Equipment

Previous steps have discussed the contributions of good shooting form and quality equipment to shooting accuracy. Matching your bow setup and arrows to your individual shooting style is a third factor that contributes to accurate scoring. Tuning is the process of adjusting equipment to perform optimally for an individual shooter. In this step you learn to make initial adjustments to your equipment, to select your arrow size, and then to tune your equipment using one of three available methods. Exercises help you practice these adjustments and a checklist is provided for recording your movement through a tuning procedure.

WHY TUNE YOUR EQUIPMENT?

Tuning involves adjustments that result in clean arrow flight and good arrow grouping. If an arrow does not fly smoothly—it wobbles or fishtails in flight—it is using energy that would otherwise contribute to increased arrow speed. Increased arrow speed brings the arrow to its target sooner, minimizing the effect of bow hand torque, a poor release, misaiming, or any other mistake on the archer's part. Ideally, tuning eliminates all wobbling of an arrow in flight.

INITIAL ADJUSTMENTS

Several determinations and decisions must be made before you actually tune your bow. These include the draw weight and tiller (string height) of the bow, arrow rest type, draw length; arrow shaft size, fletching type and size, tip weight; and the stabilizer setup. Changes in any of these factors could make it necessary to retune the bow. Some of these factors are more pertinent for recurve bows than compounds, and others are more pertinent for compounds than recurves.

Recurve Bows

The bow draw weight is needed, along with draw length, to choose arrow size. Most bow shops have a scale that gives the draw weight of a bow at any draw length. It is worthwhile to check a bow on one of these scales. Recall that bows are labeled for draw weight at a standard draw length. Yet, you want to make sure the label is correct and the appropriate adjustment is made for draw lengths longer or shorter than the standard.

It is necessary for the string height of a recurve bow (the distance between the bow's pivot point and the string) to be set before tuning. The bowstring's length fixes the string height. For straight-limb bows, a string length should be used that results in a string height from 6-8 inches. For recurve bows, the string height should be approximately 8 inches. Manufacturers typically specify a string height range for their quality recurve bows. You can adjust the string height within this range.

The sound of the bow upon release is often a good indicator of the ideal string height for a given bow and archer; the string height that results in the quietest action is the ideal one. Slight changes in string height can be achieved by twisting or untwisting the bowstring. Obviously, twisting the string shortens its length and increases the string height. The twists should always be in the same direction as the center serving. Never remove all the twists from a string. It should have 6-10 twists to keep it round and without flat spots that plane in the air upon release and slow its speed. On the other hand, the increased friction of too many twists increases the likelihood of string breakage.

As mentioned earlier, you need to know draw length and draw weight to choose arrow size. If you have not checked your draw length recently, it is wise to recheck it before purchasing arrows and tuning your bow to them. Refer to Step 1, Fitting Basic Equipment.

Select your arrow rest and install it before tuning your bow. It is best to have an arrow rest used in combination with a cushion plunger because the plunger allows both for movement of the pressure point in and out and for independent adjustment of the spring tension. The arrow rest support arm should be of the type that does not interfere with the passage of the arrow fletching or that moves freely if contacted by the fletching. It should be installed so that the center of the arrow shaft is at the center of the cushion plunger button when the shaft rests on the support arm.

Install any accessories you plan to use before tuning. These include stabilizers, a bowsight, a draw check, and a kisser button. Changes in accessories, especially those that could affect arrow clearance or weight of the bowstring, could affect the tuning.

Compound Bows

There are several initial adjustments to make before tuning a compound bow. Some are similar to those made in setting up a recurve bow; others are unique. First, you should have your compound bow set for your draw length. This should have been done at the pro shop when you purchased your bow. You can follow the instructions that came with the bow to change the draw length yourself, but this requires unscrewing the limb bolts to take all the tension off the cables. A pro shop has a bow press that allows instantaneous adjustment of the draw length.

Next, the cable guard should be adjusted and tightened if your bow is equipped with an adjustable guard. The cable guard holds the cables away from the nocked arrow so it can pass freely upon release. The cable guard should be set to route the cables just out of the way, but no further than necessary. On some compounds, changes in cable guard position slightly affect the draw length—hence the necessity to make this adjustment before tuning.

Compound bows have a draw weight range. Before setting the desired draw weight, it is necessary to adjust a compound bow's tiller. *Tiller* is the perpendicular distance between the string and each limb, measured where the limb attaches to the handle riser. Manufacturers often recommend the tiller settings for their bows. Most are such that the top limb

tiller is approximately 1/8 inch longer than the bottom limb tiller. Tiller can be measured with a bow square or metal tape (see Figure 16.1).

To change the tiller, use an Allen wrench to turn the limb bolt—clockwise to lengthen the tiller, counterclockwise to shorten it. On modern, two-wheel compound bows, just what the tiller measurements are is not as important as setting them and checking regularly to be sure they remain the same.

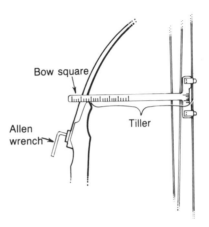

Figure 16.1   Tiller adjustment on a compound bow.

Once tiller is set on a compound bow, the draw weight can be set by using a scale and turning the limb bolts with an Allen wrench. The draw weight should be the weight you can shoot with good form over the course of a shooting round. A clockwise turn increases the poundage. Be sure to adjust the top and bottom bolts an equal number of turns to maintain the tiller ratio.

A wide range of arrow rests are available for compound bows. You should select an arrow rest before tuning. Shoot-around and shoot-through rests are available (see Step 18). Most archers using their fingers to hold and release the bowstring select a shoot-around rest. Most archers using a mechanical release aid select a shoot-through style, but this is not a definite rule.

The preferred shoot-around rest is the flexible support arm-cushion plunger combination. However, many compound bow archers use spring rests successfully. With such a rest, the arrow support arm should place the center of the arrow shaft at the center of the cushion plunger button or the spring. Shoot-through rests are available in a variety of models. Some use a cushion plunger; others do not.

As with a recurve bow, all accessories should be installed on your compound bow before tuning. These include stabilizers, a bowsight, a draw check, a kisser button, a string peep sight, and any cable keepers that

Table 16.1 Shaft Selection Chart

Directions for Using Chart: 1)Recurve Bows: Find your actual draw weight in the left hand vertical column and follow this band horizontally across to your arrow length. Arrow sizes in that block are most likely your best fit. Sizes in bold type are the most widely used. 2) Compound Bows: Determine your holding and peak weights on a bow scale, available at most pro shops. Add these weights together and divide by 2 to determine your equivalent compound bow weight. Find this value in the left hand column and use the chart as described above for recurve bows. Alternatively, determine your peak weight on a scale and consult the manufacturer's literature to find your bow's percent let-off. Find the peak weight in the appropriate right hand vertical column and use the table as described above.

EASTON ALUMINUM "QUICK REFERENCE" CHART[a]

ACTUAL RECURVE BOW WEIGHT —OR— EQUIVALENT COMPOUND BOW WEIGHT (POUNDS & KILOGRAMS)	CORRECT ARROW LENGTH (INCHES & CENTIMETERS)									COMPOUND PEAK BOW WEIGHT (POUNDS & KILOGRAMS)	
	61.0 CM. 24"	63.5 CM. 25"	66.0 CM. 26"	68.6 CM. 27"	71.1 CM. 28"	73.7 CM. 29"	76.2 CM. 30"	78.7 CM. 31"	81.3 CM. 32"	30% LET-OFF	50% LET-OFF
20-25# (9.1-11.3 KG.)	1416⊙	1516⊙⊠	**1516⊙⊠** 1518⊙	1518⊙ 1614⊠ 1616⊙⊠	**1616⊙⊠** **1714⊠**	1714⊠ 1713⊙ 1813⊙	1813⊙ **1716⊙⊠** **1814⊠** 1816⊙⊠	1913⊙		24-29# (10.9-13.2 KG.)	27-33# (12.3-15.0 KG.)
25-30# (11.3-13.6 KG.)	1516⊠	**1516⊙⊠** 1518⊙	1518⊙ **1614⊠** **1616⊙⊠**	**1616⊙⊠** 1618⊙ 1713⊙ **1714⊠**	**1714⊠** **1716⊙⊠** 1813⊙	**1716○⊠** 1813⊙ **1814⊠**	1816⊙⊠ 1913⊙	**1914⊠** 1916⊙⊠		29-35# (13.2-15.9 KG.)	33-40# (15.0-18.1 KG.)
30-35# (13.6-15.9 KG.)	**1516⊙⊠** 1518⊙	1518⊙ **1614⊠**	**1616⊙⊠** 1618⊙ 1713⊙ **1714⊠**	1618⊙ **1714⊠** **1716⊙⊠** 1813⊙	**1716⊙⊠** 1813⊙ **1814⊠**	1718⊙ **1816⊙⊠** 1913⊙	1818⊙ **1914⊠** **1916⊙⊠**	**1916⊙⊠** 2013⊙ **2014⊠**	2016⊙ 2114⊙	35-41# (15.9-18.6 KG.)	40-47# (18.1-21.3 KG.)
35-40# (15.9-18.1 KG.)	1518⊙ **1614⊠**	**1616⊙⊠** 1618⊙ 1713⊙	1618⊙ **1714⊠** **1716⊙⊠** 1813⊙	**1716⊙⊠** 1813⊙ **1814⊠**	1718⊙ **1816⊙⊠** 1913⊙	1818⊙ **1914⊠** **1916⊙⊠**	**1916⊙⊠** 2013⊙ **2014⊠**	1918⊙ 2016⊙ 2114⊙	2018⊙ **2114⊙** **2115⊠** 2213⊙	41-47# (18.6-21.3 KG.)	47-53# (21.3-24.0 KG.)
40-45# (18.1-20.4 KG.)	**1616⊙⊠** 1618⊙ 1713⊙	1618⊙ **1714⊠** **1716⊙⊠** 1813⊙	**1716⊙⊠** 1813⊙ **1814⊠**	1718⊙ **1816⊙⊠** 1913⊙	1818⊙ **1914⊠** **1916⊙⊠**	**1916⊙⊠** 2013⊙ **2014⊠**	1918⊙ **2016⊙** 2114⊙	2018⊙ **2114⊙** **2115⊠** 2213⊙	2018⊙ **2115⊠** **2213⊙**	47-53# (21.3-24.0 KG.)	53-60# (24.0-27.2 KG.)
45-50# (20.4-22.7 KG.)	1618⊙ **1714⊠** **1716⊙⊠** 1813⊙	**1716⊙⊠** 1813⊙ **1814⊠**	1718⊙ **1816⊙⊠** 1913⊙	1818⊙ **1914⊠** **1916⊙⊠**	**1916⊙⊠** 2013⊙ **2014⊠**	1918⊙ **2016⊙** 2114⊙	2018⊙ **2114⊙** **2115⊠** 2213⊙	2018⊙ **2115⊠** **2213⊙**	2117⊙ 2216⊙	53-59# (24.0-26.8 KG.)	60-67# (27.2-30.4 KG.)
50-55# (22.7-24.9 KG.)		1718⊙ **1816⊙⊠** 1913⊙	1818⊙ **1914⊠** **1916⊙⊠**	**1916⊙⊠** 2013⊙ **2014⊠**	1918⊙ **2016⊙** 2114⊙	2018⊙ **2114⊙** **2115⊠** 2213⊙	2018⊙ **2115⊠** **2213⊙**	2117⊙ 2216⊙	2216⊙	59-65# (26.8-29.5 KG.)	67-73# (30.4-33.1 KG.)
55-60# (24.9-27.2 KG.)			**1916⊙⊠** 2013⊙ **2014⊠**	1918⊙ **2016⊙** 2114⊙	2018⊙ **2114⊙** **2115⊠** 2213⊙	2018⊙ **2115⊠** **2213⊙**	2117⊙ 2216⊙	2216⊙	2219⊙	65-71# (29.5-32.2 KG.)	73-80# (33.1-36.3 KG.)

Note: 1413 not listed, should be used for draw lengths of less than 24'' (57.6 CM) and bow weights under 20 lbs.
⊙ Indicates XX75®   ⊠ Indicates X7®
2024 Alloy (24SRT-X® , Swift® & Game Getter®) not listed = 1% stiffer in spine & 1% lighter in weight than XX75® .
XX75® X7® 24SRT-X® Swift® Game Getter®   ® Reg. TM. Jas. D. Easton, Inc.
[a]The Easton Aluminum ''Quick Reference'' chart is from *Target archery with Easton aluminum shafts* (p. 9) by Easton Aluminum, Inc., 1981, Van Nuys, CA. Copyright 1981 by Jas. D. Easton, Inc. Reprinted by permission.

hold the cables in close proximity to one another.

SELECTING YOUR ARROWS

It is absolutely necessary for good shooting that you have arrows uniform in spine and weight and of the proper size. The arrow manufacturer makes available a chart listing one or more shaft sizes for a given bow draw weight and arrow length. Table 16.1 is the quick-reference chart for Easton aluminum shafts. Directions for using the chart are given, but you must know your bow draw weight, as discussed earlier, and your arrow length.

To determine your arrow length, add at least 3/4 inch to your draw length. If you're using a clicker, you should consider that your arrow length must allow for the use of the clicker. Bowhunters need extra length so that when their broadheads are installed, the blades are well in front of their bow hands.

Aluminum arrow shaft sizes are designated by four digits. The first two indicate the outside shaft diameter, measured in 64ths of an inch. The second two indicate the aluminum tube wall thickness, measured in thousandths of an inch. For example, an 1813 shaft is 18/64ths of an inch in diameter and 13/1000ths of an inch in wall thickness. As you can see from the chart, a stiffer arrow is recommended as bow draw weight increases. A heavier arrow is recommended as arrow length increases. Keep in mind that the chart gives guidelines, not definitive rules. The unique qualities of bow and archer may result in an arrow selection other than that recommended.

With some aluminum shaft alloys, you have a choice of regular or heavyweight arrow tips. Most archers experiment to find the tip weights that are best for them. A heavier tip results in heavier arrow weight, but it is usually more effective in crosswind conditions. Whichever tip is used when first tuning, changing weights necessitates retuning.

You also must decide whether to shoot arrows fletched with feathers or plastic vanes, as well as what size fletching to use. These decisions often hinge on whether you anticipate shooting indoors or out. Many archers fletch their arrows with feathers for indoor shoot-

ing and vanes for outdoor shooting, to take advantage of the strengths of each type of fletching.

Feathers are lighter and typically considered more "forgiving" than vanes. That is, they better compensate for your shooting flaws, such as a poor release. Slight contact between feathers and the arrow rest or bow window does not usually affect arrow flight as significantly as the same contact by plastic vanes.

On the other hand, feathers are affected by rain and wind. Vanes are thinner and smoother than feathers and do not slow down an arrow as rapidly as feathers do. Being uniformly produced, they typically yield better arrow grouping at longer distances.

Archers using mechanical release aids are an exception, typically using vanes for both indoor and outdoor shooting. Because an arrow does not bend very much with mechanical release of the string, the forgiveness of feathers can be sacrificed for the consistency of vanes. Also, small vanes are sufficient to stabilize the arrow in release shooting, and it is easier to obtain good arrow clearance with small vanes.

Archers generally use the smallest size fletching that can stabilize their arrows quickly. Large fletching increases the arrow weight; hence, archers do not want to use unnecessarily large fletching. Many archers like to mount their fletching on the arrow shaft at a small angle, rather than aligning precisely along the shaft's centerline (see Figure 16.2). The oncoming wind causes the arrow in flight to spin around its long axis, providing stability. This also slows down the arrow, with

Figure 16.2 Fletching on the arrow shaft can be mounted at a slight angle.

a greater angle causing faster slowing. Other archers mount their fletching straight on the shaft, preferring speed over the spinning effect.

You can experiment with the best combination for you, but be sure to tune your bow for the setup you decide upon and shoot arrows all fletched the same way. If you decide to angle the fletching and you are shooting feathers, be sure to offset the feathers so that the oncoming air contacts the rough side of the feather.

THE TUNING PROCESS

The tuning process is divided into two phases: preliminary alignment and fine tuning. In the preliminary alignment, the nock locator and cushion plunger are adjusted for proper arrow alignment. In the fine tuning process, fine corrections for alignment and adjustments of cushion plunger tension are made. There are several methods for making fine tuning adjustments.

Preliminary Alignment

Exercise 1: As the first adjustment in arrow alignment, the position of the cushion plunger should be set. On most models the shaft of the cushion plunger can be screwed in or out so that the plunger button protrudes through the bow a greater or lesser amount. Make this adjustment so that the center of the arrow shaft is 1/8-3/16 inch outside the bowstring (see Figure 16.3). When making this adjustment, sight along the bowstring toward the face of the bow. Be sure you view the arrow when the bowstring is seen centered to the

bow. On a recurve bow, the bowstring is aligned with the center of the bow limbs. On a compound bow, though, the bowstring is offset to the outside because of the eccentric pulleys. Be sure you take this into account when aligning the cushion plunger.

Exercise 2: The next phase in preliminary alignment is to position the nock locator on the bowstring so that the arrow nock is approximately 3/8 inch above the line forming a perfect 90-degree angle with the string (see Figure 16.4). This distance can be measured with a bow square (see Figure 2.2). It is ideal to use a clamp-on nock locator (see Figure 16.5). It should be clamped on firmly but not tightly at this time. In fine tuning, it can be threaded up or down to make a fine adjustment, then tightly clamped down. Caution is needed with Kevlar bowstrings not to clamp down the nock locator too tightly.

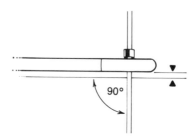

Figure 16.4 Nock locator on the bowstring.

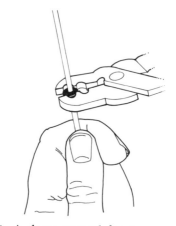

Figure 16.5 A clamp-on nock locator.

Fine Tuning

There are several methods for fine tuning. Every archer tends to prefer one over the others. It is best to experiment in order to find the one you prefer. The methods included

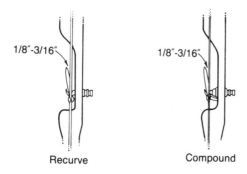

Recurve   Compound

Figure 16.3 Position of the cushion plunger on recurve and compound bows.

here are the bare shaft method, the variable distance method, and paper tuning. All of these methods are described for right-handed shooters; if you're left-handed, remember to transpose the pertinent left/right directions.

Bare Shaft Method

For bare shaft tuning, you need three fletched arrows and two or three identical arrows without fletching. The first phase of tuning is to check for porpoising of the arrow in flight, a motion wherein the nock end of the arrow appears to move up and down in flight (see Figure 16.6).

Shoot 3 fletched arrows at a target from 10 to 15 yards. Then shoot 2 or 3 unfletched, but identically aimed, arrows. If the unfletched shafts plane up on their flight to the target or hit higher on the target than the fletched shafts, move the nock locator up on the bowstring. If the unfletched shafts plane down or

make impact lower than the fletched shafts, move the nock locator down (see Figure 16.7). After an adjustment, repeat this process until the fletched and unfletched shafts hit at the same height on the target. Porpoising must be corrected before moving to the next tuning phase.

The second phase in bare shaft tuning is a check for fishtailing, wherein the nock end of the arrow appears to move from side to side in flight (see Figure 16.8). Repeat the procedure described above. If the unfletched shafts hit the target to the left of the fletched shafts, decrease the spring tension on the cushion plunger or use a weaker spring rest. Follow the manufacturer's directions to adjust the plunger (see Figure 16.9). If you do not have a cushion plunger on your bow, move the pressure point in toward the bow. Unfletched shafts hitting to the right of the fletched shafts necessitate increasing the spring tension,

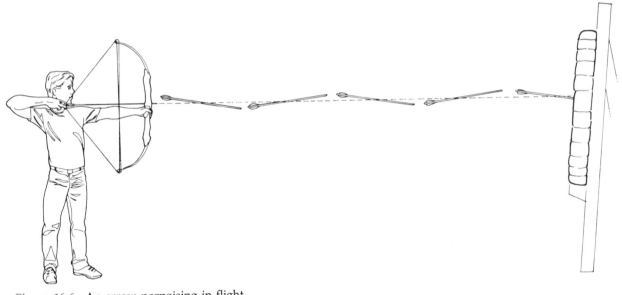

Figure 16.6   An arrow porpoising in flight.

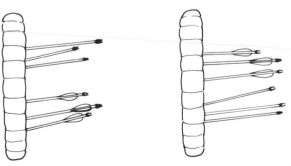

Figure 16.7   The unfletched shaft should not impact either above or below the fletched shaft.

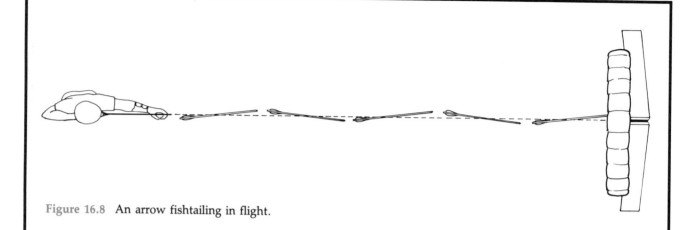

Figure 16.8 An arrow fishtailing in flight.

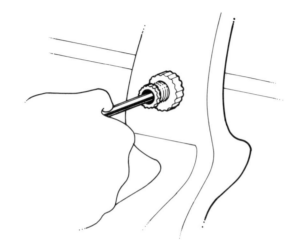

Figure 16.9 Adjusting the plunger.

using a stiffer spring rest, or moving the pressure point out (see Figure 16.10).

After each adjustment, repeat this process until you can bring the unfletched shafts to within at least 4 inches of the fletched shafts at a distance of 15 yards. If you cannot make further adjustments to bring the unfletched shafts within 4 inches, your arrow shaft size

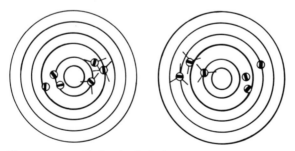

Figure 16.10 Unfletched shafts should not hit to the left or right of fletched shafts.

may have to be changed to achieve good arrow flight.

If you are shooting a compound bow, you also have the option of adjusting the bow's peak weight poundage to correct for fishtailing. If your unfletched shafts hit left of the fletched shafts, increase the poundage. If your unfletched shafts hit right, decrease the poundage. Make your adjustments in increments of approximately 1 pound, repeating the shooting procedure after each adjustment.

The final check in bare shaft tuning is a check for proper clearance of the arrow through the arrow rest and bow window. Sprinkle talcum powder on the arrow rest and bow window, or spray both the fletched end of the arrow and the arrow rest assembly with dry spray deodorant. Shoot an arrow and examine the bow. You can identify places where the arrow fletching strikes the rest or bow window. If your arrow is not clearing properly, move the cushion plunger or pressure point farther out and retune your bow for fishtailing. Also, check to be sure your bowstring is not catching on a shirt pocket, sleeve, or collar. If you cannot achieve proper clearance, you may have to change your arrow shaft size.

Some archers use only one bare shaft when they tune. If you attempt to do so, be sure you base your adjustments on bare shaft shots that are well aimed and well executed. You will spend considerably more time tuning your bow if you make an unnecessary or incorrect adjustment after a poorly executed shot with a bare shaft.

The Variable Distance Method

The variable distance tuning method requires shooting from distances of up to 35 yards. The first phase of this tuning method is to check for porpoising in the same manner described above in bare shaft tuning. Once the nocking point is set, proceed with tuning to correct fishtailing.

Establish a sight setting for 15 yards; leave the sight at this setting until tuning is completed. Place a mark near the top of the target mat. Aiming at this mark, shoot an arrow from each of the following distances: 10, 15, 20, 25, 30, and 35 yards.

Look at the pattern formed by the arrows. If the line of arrows forms the letter C (see Figure 16.11), the cushion plunger or pressure

point is protruding too far into the bow window and should be adjusted inward. If the arrows form a backward C, the cushion plunger or pressure point is too far in and should be adjusted outward. (Left-handed archers should remember to transpose these and many subsequent directions. For example, if arrows form C, plunger or point is too far in and should be adjusted outward.)

If the arrows form a diagonal line slanting to the low left, the tension of the cushion plunger or spring rest is too stiff. The cushion plunger tension should be decreased or the spring rest replaced by a lighter spring. Conversely, if the arrows form a diagonal line slanting to the low right, the cushion plunger tension should be increased or the spring rest replaced by a stiffer spring.

Adjustments should be made in small increments. Shooting should be repeated after each adjustment. When the bow is properly tuned, the arrows form a straight line down the target mat.

Paper Testing

Paper testing is a method of fine tuning that has been very successful with compound bows. In order to paper test, you need a large picture frame that can be hung 2 yards in front of a target. Newspaper is taped onto the frame. Arrows are shot through the paper and the pattern of the tear is used to make tuning adjustments.

A shooting distance of 3-8 yards is used for paper tuning. You may want to start close and, when the results look good, move back to make even finer adjustments. Archers using their fingers to hold and release typically stay within 5 yards. Archers using release aids may want to back up as far as 8 yards. The tears are the largest at approximately 8 yards.

Before paper testing, you should check for proper clearance of the fletching as it passes the arrow rest and handle riser. As described above, spray talcum powder or dry deodorant on the arrow fletching, the arrow rest, and handle riser. Shoot an arrow, then look for evidence that the fletching contacted the arrow rest or handle riser. Slight contact can sometimes be corrected by rotating the arrow nock.

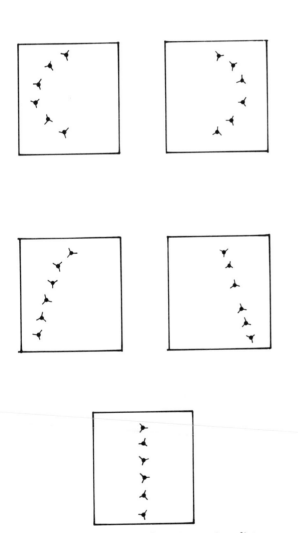

Figure 16.11 Arrows shot from increasing distances form various patterns.

Severe contact can result from a nock that fits too tightly on the string, from torquing the bowstring with the draw fingers, or from an arrow that is too stiff. Experiment with a different size nock and your hand position. If one or both of these do not correct the problem, you may need to change arrow sizes.

As with the other tuning methods, the first adjustment is for porpoising. Shoot several fletched arrows through the paper. The ideal tear pattern is a perfect hole or a hole that shows the arrow went through slightly nock-high or slightly nock-high and left for a right-hander (see Figure 16.12). If the hole indicates

Figure 16.12   Ideal tear patterns for right-handed shooters.

the arrow went through paper with the nock 3/4 inch or more high, move the nock locator down. If the arrow goes through the paper nock-down, move the nock locator up (see Figure 16.13). It is perfectly acceptable for the arrow to be slightly nock-high at this point in arrow flight because this means it is probably not hitting the rest as it passes the handle riser.

Figure 16.13   The tear pattern produced by an arrow flying nock down. The fletching tears are below the hole made by the arrow tip.

The next adjustment is for fishtailing. If a right-handed archer shoots arrows tearing holes with the nock left (see Figure 16.14), the arrows are weak in spine. The cushion plunger tension can be increased or a heavier spring rest used. The draw weight can be decreased

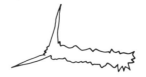

Figure 16.14   The tear pattern produced by an arrow flying nock left.

on a compound bow. The cushion plunger or pressure point can be moved in or out; but on a compound bow, it is more likely that a change in arrow size is necessary if draw weight or plunger tension adjustments do not improve the tear pattern.

If a right-handed archer shoots arrows tearing nock right (see Figure 16.15), the arrows are too stiff. The first correction tried should be an increase in the draw weight of a compound bow. Cushion plunger tension can also be decreased. It may help to move the plunger in or out. If these corrections do not improve the tear pattern, a last resort before changing arrow shaft size is to change to another type of arrow rest, one that causes arrows to tear less to the right.

Figure 16.15   The tear pattern produced by an arrow flying nock right.

As with the other methods of tuning, make adjustments in small increments and shoot several arrows through paper to check the effect of your adjustment. The ideal pattern is a perfect hole or a hole slightly nock-high and left for a right-handed shooter, nock-high and right for a left-hander.

THE FINAL PHASE

The ultimate test to check your tuning is shooting arrows to see that they group well. It is preferable to start at a short distance of approximately 20 yards and work back to the longest distance you plan to shoot. Of course, you must consider your skill level in judging the size of your groups.

You need to work through some of the phases in the tuning process again if your arrows do not group at the distances you plan to shoot. Generally, if your groups spread horizontally, your nocking point may still be slightly low, your cushion plunger too stiff, or both. If your groups spread vertically, your nocking point may be slightly high, your cushion plunger too soft, or both. However, you must not be afraid to experiment with any of your adjustments.

Occasionally, archers find that the tuning setup that produces the best groups is not the one that produces the most smoothly flying arrows. In the majority of cases, though, smooth arrow flight and tight groups go hand in hand.

A kisser button or peep sight may need minor adjustments in its position after tuning.

This is necessitated by changes in the position of the nocking point in the fine tuning process.

There are a few additional changes you can make if tuning problems persist. If an arrow is too stiff (a bare shaft hits left of fletched arrows) and cushion plunger and draw weight adjustments do not seem to correct the problem, perhaps a longer arrow, heavier arrow tips, or increased string height will help. If an arrow is too weak in spine, try a shorter arrow, a lighter arrow tip, a shorter string height, or adding mass weight to your bow.

As you can see, tuning requires time and patience. You must be willing to experiment, seeing what effect an adjustment has on arrow flight. Try to make just one adjustment at a time, shooting after each change. This obviously requires time, but you will be rewarded in the end by knowing that your equipment is contributing its utmost to your scoring accuracy.

Tuning Practice Drills

You may not be able to adjust the bow with which you are presently shooting because it is school or borrowed equipment. It is valuable experience to practice tuning, however—both for the knowledge gained about the workings of bows and arrows and for the possibility that you will have your own bow to tune in the future.

1. Arrow Selection Practice

It is important to select the appropriate aluminum arrow shaft size to shoot accurately. Practice selecting an arrow shaft for each of the following bow weights and draw lengths from Table 16.1. Write your selection in the space provided, giving both the shaft size and the aluminum alloy (e.g., X7, XX75, etc.).

Success Goal = to select every arrow shaft accurately

Your Choices =

Recurve Bow

For 35 pounds, 29 inches: _____

For 22 pounds, 26 inches: _____

For 27 pounds, 27 inches: _____

For 40 pounds, 30 inches: _____

Compound Bow

For 35 pounds, 50% letoff, 27 inches: _____

For 43 pounds, 50% letoff, 29 inches: _____

For 47 pounds, 50% letoff, 31 inches: _____

For 50 pounds, 50% letoff, 30 inches: _____

2. Clearance Test

Spray talcum powder on the fletched end of one of your arrows, your arrow rest, and your bow window. Shoot the arrow into a target at close range. Check for contact of the fletching with the rest or bow window. Describe your findings below and the adjustment you could make to correct any unwanted contact.

Success Goal = to correctly identify the adjustment needed to obtain arrow clearance

Your Results =

Describe any contact you found:

_____

_____

Describe an adjustment you would make based on your findings if this were your own equipment:

_____

_____

3. Tuning Mimic

In this exercise, identify an adjustment that could be made in your archery equipment if you obtained the result specified in the tuning process given.

Success Goal = to correctly identify the adjustment needed in every tuning situation

Your Results =

a. In the variable distance method, you obtain an arrow pattern in the form of a backward **C**.

Adjustment: _____

_____

b. In the variable distance method, you obtain an arrow pattern that is a diagonal line slanting to the low left.

Adjustment: _____

_____

c. In bare shaft tuning, the unfletched shafts hit the target left of the fletched shafts.

Adjustment: _____

_____

d. In bare shaft tuning, the unfletched shafts hit below the fletched shafts.

Adjustment: _____

_____

e. In paper tuning, the arrow tears the paper with the nock 1 inch high.

Adjustment: _____

_____

4. Porpoising Test

Use the paper tuning method described in this step to test for porpoising. At the right, sketch the paper tear obtained.

Variation: Use one of the other tuning methods.

Success Goal = to identify the adjustments needed to correct porpoising

Your Results =

Describe what, if any, adjustment you would make of the nock locator position, based on your findings:

_____

_____

5. *Fishtailing Test*

Assume that you have corrected for porpoising. Use the paper tuning method to test for fishtailing. At the right, sketch the tear pattern you obtained.

Variation: Use one of the other tuning methods.

Success Goal = to identify the adjustments needed to correct for fishtailing

Your Results =

Describe an adjustment you would make, based on your findings:

_____

_____

Tuning
Keys to Success Checklist

Tuning involves many different settings and adjustments. It is easy to lose track of where you are in the tuning process. Yet, it is important that some of the adjustments be made in sequence. The following checklist can help you proceed through the tuning process. Check each key as you make an adjustment or selection (see Suggested Readings for additional information).

Pretuning
Adjustments

_____ Draw length adjustment (compounds)

_____ Cable guard adjustment (compounds)

_____ Tiller setting (compounds)

_____ Draw weight setting

_____ String height adjustment (recurves)

_____ Arrow rest installation

_____ Bowsight and accessory installation

Arrow
Selection

_____ Arrow length

_____ Arrow shaft size

_____ Arrow tip weight selection

_____ Arrow fletching selection

Preliminary
Alignment

_____ Center-shot alignment

_____ Nock locator positioning

**Fine
Tuning**

____ Fletch clearance (paper testing)   ____ Fishtailing

____ Porpoising   ____ Fletch clearance (bare shaft test)

**Final
Testing**

____ Grouping at short distances   ____ Grouping at long distances

____ Grouping at intermediate distances

Suggested Readings

Easton Aluminum. (1981). *Target archery with Easton aluminum shafts*. Van Nuys, CA.

Wise, L. (1985). *On target for tuning your compound bow*. Mequon, WI: Target Communications.

Step 17 Maintaining Your Equipment

You are responsible for seeing that your archery equipment is in safe shooting condition. Beyond this, properly maintained equipment shoots more efficiently and contributes to shooting accuracy. Some equipment maintenance is best undertaken by an expert, but you can learn to maintain much of your equipment.

WHY MAINTAIN YOUR EQUIPMENT YOURSELF?

In many cases, it is more economical to work on your equipment yourself than to take it to a pro shop. For example, you can often purchase a dozen nocks for the price a pro shop charges to replace one nock. You can save money by doing the simpler maintenance yourself and leaving the maintenance requiring special tools and expertise to the staff of a pro shop.

You also learn more about your equipment when you maintain it yourself. You can see how changing a setup affects shooting. Then you can better individualize your equipment to match your shooting style.

MAINTAINING YOUR ARROWS

Straight nocks are important to shooting accuracy. A nock misaligned by a few thousandths of an inch can send an arrow 6 inches off its mark at 40 yards.

Replacing Nocks

Archers who shoot tight arrow groups often break the plastic nocks on the end of their arrows. It is worthwhile to purchase replacements in quantity and a tube of fletching cement so that you can replace your own nocks. Nocks vary in size according to the size of the arrow shaft. Table 17.1 lists the appropriate size of nock to purchase for your arrows.

Table 17.1   Replacement Nock Sizes

Aluminum shafts		Fiberglass shafts	
Shaft size	Recommended nock size	Shaft size	Recommended nock size
1413 to 1518	7/32	1	1/4
1614 to 1816	1/4	2 to 4	9/32
1818 to 2016	9/32	5 to 7	5/16
2018 to 2219	5/16	8 & up	11/32
2317 to 2419	11/32		

To replace a nock, first use a knife to remove any pieces of the old nock still in place. Lightly scrape, or sand with fine grade sandpaper, any of the old cement remaining on the taper of the arrow. Because repeated scraping can distort the arrow's taper, an alternative is to carefully heat the old nock. (Do not place the arrow *in* an open flame.) When the nock begins to melt, remove it with pliers. It is best to wipe this area with acetone, methyl ethyl ketone (MEK), or metal conditioner to get a good bond. Avoid touching this area, because your fingers tend to deposit oil on the shaft.

Place a drop of fletching cement on the taper. Rotate the shaft as you spread the cement evenly around the arrow with your finger. Now place the new nock on the arrow and turn it several times counterclockwise to further spread the cement. Rotate the nock clockwise with slight downward pressure and align it approximately at right angles to the index feather (see Figure 17.1). Wipe off excess cement oozing from under the nock.

Place the arrow on a table with the index feather up. If the nock is on properly, you should not see either side of the nock when you look directly down on it from above. Adjust the nock if necessary before the cement sets. This is the standard nock position. Some archers, though, rotate their nocks slightly to

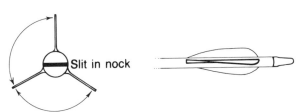

Figure 17.1   Arrow nock, cross-section and mounted on shaft.

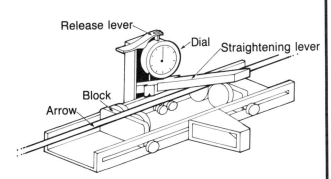

Figure 17.2   An arrow straightener.

achieve feather or vane clearance of the bow if they do not get the effect they desire with the standard position.

Another test of nock straightness is to roll the shaft on a smooth table with the fletching hanging off the table. Watch the nock to make sure its rotation doesn't have a wobbly appearance. You can also test nock straightness by resting the shaft on the fingernails of your thumb and middle finger with the arrow point against the palm of your other hand and blowing against the fletching. The arrow will spin, so you can watch for any wobbling of the nock. Adjust the nock if necessary before the cement sets. Stand the arrow up to allow the cement to dry.

Straightening Your Aluminum Arrows

Straight arrows are as important to shooting accuracy as straight nocks. Aluminum shafts can be straightened on any of several commercial straighteners if they are not too severely bent. Most pro shops make a straightener available to their customers.

Arrow straighteners have two adjustable blocks with two ball bearing wheels each. The arrow rests in the trough created by the two wheels (see Figure 17.2). For slight bends, leave the blocks at the ends of the straightener. With sharp bends or bends near the end of the shaft, move the blocks closer together. Raise the plunger and place the arrow underneath it and in the trough of each block. Starting at the point end, rotate the arrow with your index finger, being sure to position your finger on the arrow directly over the wheels in either one of the blocks. Repeat this, moving the arrow through the straightener until you reach the fletched end.

If at any point the needle on the straightener's dial scale swings more than two lines, the arrow should be straightened. Find the place on the arrow shaft yielding the most needle deflection by rotating the arrow until the needle swings the greatest amount in the clockwise direction. The peak of the bend is now uppermost. Press down on the straightening lever. Rotate the arrow to see if the bend has been removed. If not, repeat the process. When the needle deflection remains within two lines on the scale, the arrow is straightened.

Arrow straightness is so important that you should check your arrows frequently. When you are away from a straightener or on the range after scoring, there is a rough method for checking your arrows. Put the fingernails of your thumb and middle finger together. Rest the arrow shaft below the fletching on the fingernails, with the arrow point resting in your other palm. Blow on the fletching. If the shaft jumps on your fingernails, rather than spinning smoothly, the shaft may have a bend.

Replacing a Target Point

It is easy to replace a target point in aluminum arrows, but care must be taken not to subject the shaft to excessive heat in melting the cement that holds the point in place. A small gas flame, propane torch, or alcohol burner can be used. Hold the shaft above, not in, the flame until the old target point can be pulled from the arrow shaft with pliers.

First, apply enough heat to the aluminum shaft to melt a ring of ferrule cement just inside the shaft by holding the cement stick to the shaft and turning it. Immediately insert a new point about 1/2 inch into the shaft. Now heat the point and melt a layer of cement on the entire point shank. Continue to heat the point and about 1 inch of the shaft. While the cement is fluid, push the point in all the way with a workbench top or piece of wood (see Figure 17.3). Wipe off the excess glue on a piece of leather or cardboard.

Figure 17.3   Melt a layer of cement on the entire point shaft.

To remove a tip, heat the tip and lower shaft until the point can be pulled out with a pair of pliers while you twist the shaft. Replacement points must be purchased for both the exact size of shaft you are using and the grade of aluminum alloy. For better alloys, you have a choice of two point weights. The advantages of each are discussed in Step 16, Tuning Your Bow.

To replace a tip on a wood arrow, it is necessary only to heat the tip, not the wood shaft. The tip slips off of, and onto, the beveled tip of the wood shaft.

Cutting Arrow Shafts

Aluminum and tubular fiberglass shafts may be cut to your draw length. However, they are best cut with a high-speed, abrasive wheel, cutoff tool. Other methods, such as cutting with a hacksaw or rotary tube cutter, leave a rough surface that does not match flush with the target point. If you do not have access to a high-speed tool, you may want to have your arrows cut at a pro shop. Most shops provide this service if you purchase your arrows there.

Fletching Arrows

Fletching your arrows is enjoyable and provides an opportunity for you to customize and personalize your arrows. A fletching jig is needed to do the job well, though, and you may decide you will not fletch arrows often enough to justify the expense of a fletching jig.

You can obtain feathers or vanes in quantity, selecting the size and color you prefer. The advantages of each type of fletching are discussed in Step 16, Tuning Your Equipment. You also need a tube of fletching cement. Note that a jig consists of a clamp to hold the fletching, and an arrow holder that can rotate the shaft (see Figure 17.4). Consult the directions for the jig you are using.

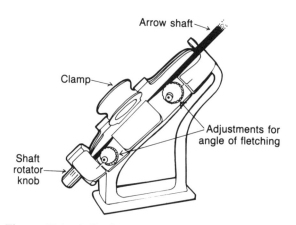

Figure 17.4   A fletching jig.

Let's assume here that you want to mount three feathers or vanes 120 degrees apart. First, you must prepare your arrow shaft properly to get a good bond between the cement and the shaft surface. If you are using regular fletching cement, wipe down the upper shaft with MEK or lacquer thinner on a paper towel, or scrub the upper shaft with an Ajax-type cleanser, rinse, and dry. If you are using a fast-drying (in 3 minutes) cement, wipe down the shaft with a mild solution of baking soda and water. If you are fletching plastic vanes, wipe down the spine of each with MEK or lacquer thinner.

Without touching the fletching area, place the shaft into the jig. Place the fletching in the jig clamp. The position of the fletching is variable, so determine how far from the nock end of the arrow you want your fletching, then mark the clamp. Place every feather or vane in the clamp at the same position. Apply a thin line of glue to the spine of the fletching, being careful not to leave a gap in the cement anywhere along the spine. Any cement spilling onto the clamp itself should be wiped away. Place the clamp in the jig, pushing the fletching all the way against the arrow shaft.

When the cement has dried, open and remove the clamp, rotate the shaft and repeat the process. Note that most jigs have an index position, marking the position where the odd-colored fletching is attached. When you have attached all three feathers or vanes, remove the arrow and place a small drop of glue at each end of each fletching. This minimizes chances of the fletching being torn from the shaft and prevents scratches from the spines of some feathers.

If you are fletching turkey feathers, be aware that they come as either right-hand wing or left-hand wing feathers. As such, they differ in which side is smooth and which is rough. Which wing feather you use, though, is not as important as being sure never to mix them on the same arrow or in the same set of arrows you are shooting. Also, should you be placing your feathers at a slight angle (see Step 16, Tuning Your Equipment), the angle should be in the direction such that the "oncoming" air moving past an arrow in flight meets the rough side of the feather, the side corresponding to the underside of a wing.

Take care of your arrows, because they greatly influence shooting accuracy. If arrows become wet, wipe them off before storing them. If feathers become wet, let them dry somewhere the feathers will not be matted down; otherwise, feathers can be steamed to regain much of their original shape. Arrows still shoot true with a small part of a feather missing or frayed. If half of a feather is torn away, though, it should be replaced. Holes in plastic vanes can be trimmed by making a V-cut into the vane. One or two small cuts still permit true arrow flight (see Figure 17.5).

Figure 17.5 Holes in plastic vanes, made by other arrows shooting through them, can be trimmed with a V-cut.

Always store arrows in an arrow case or standing on end. This keeps arrows from warping, particularly important with wood shafts.

MAINTAINING YOUR BOW

Most bows shoot well for years if properly maintained. One key in maintaining a bow is to remember that laminated bows have layers of materials that are glued together. Extreme heat, such as in a closed car on a hot, sunny day, can affect the glues used in manufacturing a bow. So, too, can prolonged exposure to moisture. Never lay a bow in damp grass. If you shoot a bow in a rain shower, wipe it dry when you finish shooting. A bow wax or other wax used frequently helps protect the bow. Solid fiberglass bows can withstand heat and moisture better than laminated bows, but extremes should still be avoided.

Recurve and straight-limb bows should be unstrung for any month that they will not be shot. Storing them in the relaxed position helps maintain their strength. It is better to string and unstring a bow with a bowstringer, rather than by hand, because stringers put equal tension on both limbs and do not twist the limbs.

Compound bows should remain strung, though. Their limbs are not under as much tension as those of a strung recurve or straight-limb bow because the eccentric pulley does much of the work. However, it is desirable to reduce the poundage of a compound bow by screwing the limb bolts out if it is going to be stored for a long period of time.

It is preferable to store bows in a case lying flat or hung vertically. In these positions neither limb takes more pressure than the other. Standing a bow in a corner eventually weakens the lower limb.

Compound bows may need to be lubricated periodically. Usually the bow manufacturer gives specific instructions on how to do this and what lubricant to use. Most pro shops also provide this service. It is also necessary to have the cables on a compound bow replaced periodically. Archers shooting four or more times per week often replace their cables every 12-18 months.

Bowstrings

Bowstrings deserve your attention. Breaking a string can cost you points in competition because the arrow may not score well or at all. Wax your bowstrings frequently with a bowstring wax; this minimizes fraying and wards off moisture. Waxed strings are also less likely to tangle when not in use. To wax a string, simply rub the wax on the string once or twice, then run your fingers up and down the string for a few minutes to distribute it evenly.

It is not necessary to wax the serving on a bowstring. Loose serving, though, should be replaced. If the serving begins to fray during a tournament or shooting session, it can be tied off temporarily and replaced later.

Tournament archers always carry one or more backup strings with them. Because new strings stretch slightly when they are first put on a bow, the well-prepared archer will have "shot in" the backup strings, that is, shot them for a practice session or two (broken them in). The tournament archer who uses strings made of Kevlar often keeps a log of how many shots have been taken with a string. Kevlar is known for its speed, but it breaks sooner than a Dacron string. So, be-fore a tournament, the archer replaces a Kevlar string he or she knows is likely to break soon.

Replacing an Arrow Rest

Arrow rests must be replaced periodically because they become worn or broken. It is critical to good equipment performance that the new rest be placed in the proper location. If your bow is equipped with a cushion plunger, you must adjust the height of the new rest so that the center of your arrow shaft contacts the center of the cushion plunger. Adjust your arrow rest in the forward/backward direction so that your arrow contacts the rest below the cushion plunger.

If your bow does not have a cushion plunger, you should install an arrow rest that has a pressure point made of a flexible material, such as plastic. Place the arrow rest so that the pressure point is located directly above the pivot point of the bow (see Figure 17.6). Varying from this point either forward or backward usually magnifies the effect of poor bow hand position and torque caused by the bow hand.

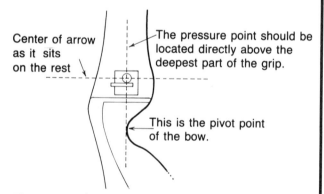

Figure 17.6 An arrow rest positioned on bow.

Practice Drills

1. Selecting a Nock Size

Below is a list of both aluminum and fiberglass arrow shaft sizes. Use Table 17.1 to find the appropriately sized nock for the shaft size given and record your choice in the blank.

Success Goal = to correctly identify the replacement nock size for each shaft listed

Your Results =

Shaft Type Size:	Nock Type Size:
Aluminum, 1616	_____
Fiberglass, 5	_____
Aluminum, 1816	_____
Fiberglass, 2	_____
Aluminum, 2018	_____
Aluminum, 1714	_____

2. Replacing a Nock

Obtain some replacement nocks for your arrows. Remove the nocks from several of your arrows and replace them, using a fletching cement, as described in this step. When finished, test them for straightness as described.

Success Goal = to replace 3 nocks and demonstrate their straightness

Your Score = (#) _____ straight replacements

3. Straightening an Arrow

If you are shooting with aluminum arrows, locate an arrow straightener. Most archery pro shops make one available for customer use. Place your arrows one by one in the straightener and straighten them.

Success Goal = to straighten all your arrows

Your Score = (#) _____ straightened arrows

4. Replacing a Target Point

Take one of your aluminum arrows and remove its point by heating the end of the arrow and pulling the point out with a pair of pliers. Remember not to get the aluminum shaft too hot. Using an appropriate cement, replace the point.

Success Goal = to replace a target point in an aluminum arrow so that it cannot be pulled out

Your Result = (check one)

_____ The arrow point came out when pulled

_____ The arrow point remained when pulled

5. Cleaning Arrow Shafts

Obtain an old aluminum arrow that you can use to practice removing fletching. With a knife, carefully scrape off the old fletching and as much of the old fletching cement as possible. Now clean the shaft as described in this step.

Success Goal = to clean an aluminum arrow shaft down to the bare aluminum

Your Results = Describe the condition of your cleaned arrow shaft: _____

_____

6. Fletching an Arrow

If you have access to an arrow fletcher, fletch the arrow you have cleaned in Drill 5. Obtain some fletching cement and 3 feathers or plastic vanes. Following the directions that come with the fletching jig place each feather or vane so that they are equally spaced on the shaft. (Use the fletching cement sparingly.) Let dry.

Success Goal = to fletch an arrow with the feathers or vanes equally spaced

Your Results = View your arrow from the nock end. Are the feathers or vanes equally spaced? _____ Does the fletching come off when pulled? _____

Step 18 Upgrading Your Equipment

Basic equipment is adequate while you are learning basic shooting form. Form is the biggest variable in shooting accuracy at this stage of acquiring archery skill. Once good form is established and made consistent from shot to shot, though, there is benefit from investing in better equipment and more accessories. This step shows you how to upgrade your equipment. Notice that it does not include drills or exercises. In some cases, upgrading your equipment is simply a matter of purchasing an accessory and using it as you continue to shoot. It may be some time before you are able to upgrade your equipment. In this event, this step serves as a reference to which you can come back in the future.

WHY UPGRADE YOUR EQUIPMENT?

Consistency from shot to shot has been emphasized over and over again during your learning of basic form. Just as it is important for you to be consistent, so must your archery equipment be consistent. Better equipment, made of better materials and taking advantage of the latest technological advances, tends to perform more consistently for you. There are also accessories that help both you and your equipment perform even more consistently.

UPGRADING YOUR ARROWS

It is often said that if you give a skilled archer a choice between quality arrows and a basic bow on the one hand, and basic arrows and a quality bow on the other, the archer would choose quality arrows and a basic bow—so important are good arrows to accurate shooting! The best arrows are those that are consistent in the degree they bend when stressed a specified amount. This quality is called *spine*.

To see why spine is so important, it is necessary to understand how an arrow clears the bow when you release the bowstring. First,

consider what happens to the bowstring when you release it. Even with the cleanest of releases, the bowstring rolls off your fingertips and tab, sending it slightly in toward you as it moves forward. It then rebounds away from you, then again slightly toward you as it reaches brace height. The string, being attached to the limbs, reaches its limit of forward movement and reverses directions, moving slightly away, then oscillating at brace height (see Figure 18.1).

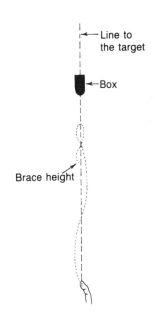

Figure 18.1 String path after release.

The arrow, of course, is attached to the bowstring at release, so the nock end of the arrow moves slightly toward your chest with the bowstring. At the same time, the full forward force of the bow's stored energy is transferred through the string to the arrow. The point end of the arrow, resting against the bow, pushes outward against it. The bow resists this push. The arrow center is free to bend between these two pressure points. It first bends slightly to the right of a direct line to the target (see

Figure 18.2). As the arrow continues forward, the center of the shaft bends to the left, in an "equal and opposite reaction" to the first bend. Hence the shaft is bending around the bow handle. Just as the fletching approaches the bow handle, the shaft bends to the right once more, moving the fletching away from the arrow rest and bow handle. In effect, the arrow bends around the bow without touching it. This is often termed the *archer's paradox*. The arrow continues toward the target, alternately bending right and left in decreasing amounts until it straightens out about 10 yards in front of the bow, flying on line to the target.

The initial push of the arrow tip on the bow handle at release causes the bow to move slightly. Stabilizers, which are discussed later in this step, help to retard this bow movement.

It is important for arrows to have two qualities, in light of how they clear the bow. First, the amount of bend, or arrow spine, must be

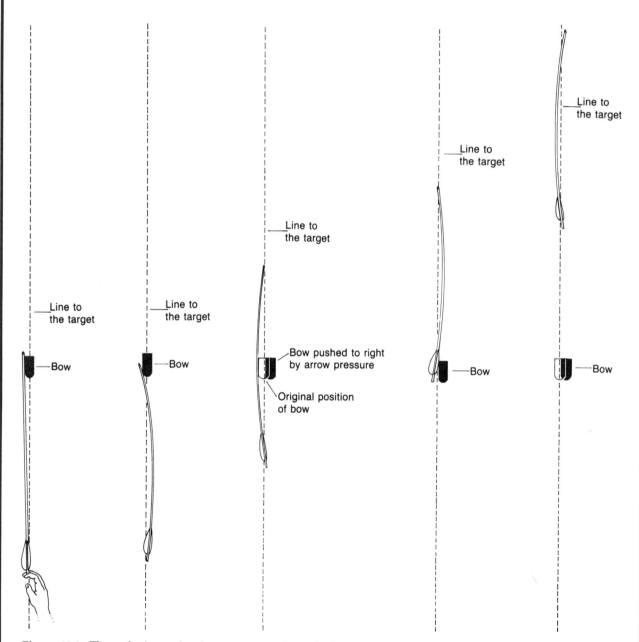

Figure 18.2 The *archer's paradox*: how an arrow clears the bow.

just right for your draw length and bow weight. That is, arrow spine must be matched to you and the bow so that the archer's paradox results in the arrow fletching clearing the bow handle without contact. Attaining this match is addressed in Step 16. Second, every arrow you shoot must have the same spine. Arrows do not group in the same place on the target, no matter how good your form, unless their spine, the way they bend around the bow, is identical.

The arrows least consistent in spine are wood, because there is no way to obtain identical wood for each shaft. Fiberglass arrows are more consistent than wood, but aluminum arrows are undoubtedly the best choice. Not only can they be made to a standard, but aluminum shafts vary in both diameter and wall thickness to create a wider variety of sizes. You can be very selective in matching arrow spine to your draw length and weight.

Aluminum shafts are available in several alloys. The most expensive varieties are the strongest and do not bend as easily as others. Most competitive target archers today use one of the two top-grade aluminum alloys. Even if you do not compete, you may want to invest in arrows of this quality for both their consistency and their durability.

Some competitive archers use an aluminum arrow wrapped with a thin layer of carbon fibers. This type of arrow allows you to use a lighter, stiffer shaft, which is faster and more resistant to wind than an aluminum arrow. Its chief advantage comes in outdoor shooting at long distances. Competitive archers in tournaments of this type find it well worthwhile to invest in aluminum-carbon arrows.

You can choose from a variety of arrow nock styles (see Figure 18.3). Which one you use is a matter of preference, but it should be a snap-on nock. A snap-on nock lightly holds the arrow on the bowstring and minimizes the chances of a dry fire (releasing the string with the arrow having slipped off).

UPGRADING YOUR BOW

If you are serious about participating in some form of archery, you should have your own

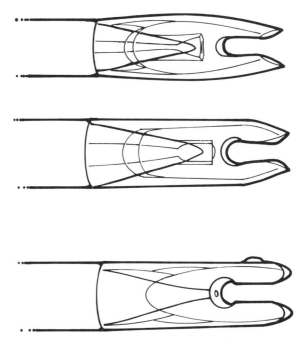

Figure 18.3 A variety of arrow nock styles.

bow. The bow itself can be matched to you for draw weight and for bow or draw length. Also, the bow can be set up, or tuned, specifically for your needs. A good rule of thumb is to buy the best bow affordable, commensurate with your interest in the sport.

An important consideration in purchasing a bow is to look for a bow that is "center shot." A center-shot bow has a bow window cut into the handle and allows the drawn arrow to sit at a point close to or at the centerline of the limbs. A bow without a window puts the arrow in a position where it is pointed significantly to the side. Even allowing for the archer's paradox effect of the arrow bending around the bow, an archer with a bow without a window must aim allowing for the arrow to fly off-center. A center-shot bow overcomes this problem. An arrow of appropriate spine can compensate for the slight offset from center by the archer's paradox effect.

Center-shot bows must necessarily either be wood bows that are laminated, usually with layers of fiberglass on the face and back of the bow, or be bows with metal handle risers. A simple wood bow would not be strong enough if a bow window were cut into the handle. Most quality bows today have metal handle risers, often made of magnesium, because they are thus strong enough to withstand the forces to which they are subjected in shooting even when cut exactly center shot (see Figure 18.4). Both recurve and compound bows are found with metal handle risers.

Bows with metal handle risers have detachable limbs that can be of a variety of materials. Most have a wood core and a layer of fiberglass on both sides. Higher quality limbs can have multilaminated wood cores (see Figure 18.5). The fiberglass layers provide strength, durability, and shooting speed. Through modern technology, bow manufacturers are able to offer bow limbs of other materials as well. These include limbs with carbon layers, with foam cores, and of solid fiberglass. Each has its advantages and disadvantages. A relatively new archer considering a purchase

should ask about these advantages and disadvantages with an eye toward consistent performance and durability.

Bows with detachable limbs allow you to replace the limbs without having to purchase an entirely new bow. Recurve bows can be taken apart for easy transportation, too, and frequently are called *take-down* bows for this reason. Compound bows are usually left assembled, but the advantage of this metal riser-limb construction is that the angle of the limbs can be adjusted by turning the limb bolt. This allows the draw weight of a compound to be adjusted, typically through a 15-pound range.

Most bowstrings are made of Dacron strands. The number of strands is related to the bow's draw weight. A string of 8 strands is sufficient for 20-30 pound bows, 10 strands for 25-35 pound bows, 12 strands for 35-45

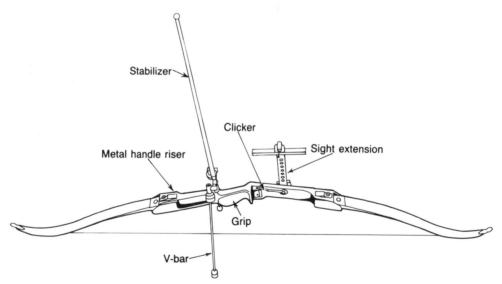

Figure 18.4 Bow with a metal handle riser.

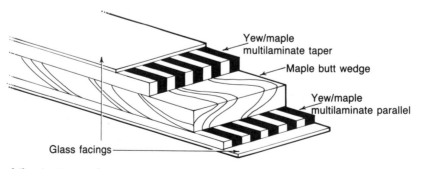

Figure 18.5 A multilaminate wood core.

pound bows, 14 strands for 45-55 pound bows, and 16 strands for bows over 55 pounds. Choose a string with the number of strands appropriate for your poundage. Remember that more strands means a larger diameter. If you have a bow relatively light in poundage and arrows matched to it, your arrow nocks will probably be too tight on a bowstring with significantly more strands than you need. Obviously, though, selecting a string with too few strands puts you at greater risk of breaking a bowstring.

Dacron strings stretch slightly when first used. Bowstrings made of Kevlar are also available. They do not stretch as much as Dacron and are very strong, but they also cost more and do not last as long. Among prudent archers the use of Kevlar bowstrings requires keeping track of how many times the string has been shot, so that it can be replaced before it breaks.

Bowstrings are *served*, or reinforced, at the loops and in the middle where the arrow is nocked and you hold the string. The center serving should be as long as it needs to be for protection from wear—but no longer, to save weight and maintain the highest string speed possible on release. Nylon and monofilament are the two most common materials used for the center serving. Monofilament does not fray like nylon but unravels quickly if it loosens or breaks.

Bowstrings are made in standard lengths. The manufacturer's suggested lengths can be used, but many experienced archers like to have their strings custom-made at a length slightly longer or shorter. The bowstring length should allow for a proper brace height. Adjusting this height is addressed in Step 16.

Adding Stabilizers

One of the first accessories you should add to your bow is a stabilizer. This is simply a metal rod with a weight on its end (see Figure 18.4). High-quality bows come with inserts allowing one or more stabilizers to be attached to the face or back of the bow.

A stabilizer is beneficial to shooting accuracy because it reduces the tendency of the bow to torque in the bow hand. If you think back to the discussion of the archer's paradox, you remember that the arrow pushes against the bow handle when the string is released. This push causes the bow to turn about its long axis. By placing a weight away from the axis of rotation, the rotation is slowed and minimized, allowing the arrow to clear the bow handle before it can be seriously affected by the turning bow handle. The farther a given weight is from the axis of rotation or the heavier the weight, the greater its effect in reducing torque. If you prefer a setup lighter in weight, you can use a lighter weight farther from the axis. If you don't mind the heavy weight, you can use a shorter stabilizer rod. Hence, you have many possible combinations of stabilizer lengths and weights in addition to the number of stabilizers.

Exactly what combination of stabilization is ideal is a topic of discussion among archers. You must find the setup that works best for your shooting. A reasonable beginning is to add a single stabilizer with a moderate weight to the back of the bow below the grip so that the stabilizer rod extends toward the target; a length of 30-33 inches is sufficient. Another common stabilizer setup is to attach V-bars at the same location (see Figure 18.4). These bars angle back toward the archer and slightly out, forming a V-shape.

Keep in mind that the stabilizer and weight add to the weight of the bow, which must be held up and steady throughout the shot. It is best to develop strength in the bow shoulder by shooting first without a stabilizer, then adding it when sufficient strength is acquired. This rationale should also be used when increasing the weight at the end of the stabilizer or adding more stabilizers.

The Arrow Rest

For relatively little cost, you can add to the accuracy of shooting by upgrading your arrow rest (see Figure 18.6). This is particularly so if you have been shooting off the bow shelf itself. It is ideal to have a cushion plunger or spring mounted on the bow window to absorb some of the force of the arrow when the string is released and the arrow pushes aginst the bow. The cushion plunger allows an almost infinite number of settings. Springs typically come in one of several weights (see Figure 18.6d). The cushion plunger can also be adjusted as to how far from the bow window it protrudes, allowing you to adjust the arrow in this plane as well. Step 16 discusses the adjustment of these settings.

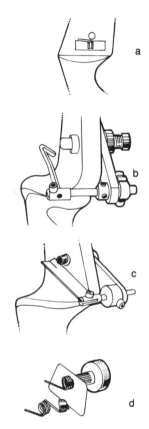

Figure 18.6 Four types of arrow rests.

Arrow rests preferably are flexible. Some are spring-loaded, collapsing against the bow window if touched by the arrow or arrow fletching as it clears the bow window. The arrow passes to the side of the support arm of such a rest. The arm then pops back to its starting position (see Figure 18.6a).

There are also arrow rests available that require the bottom fletch of the arrow to pass between the arrow support arm and the handle riser. These "shoot-through" rests are typically used by archers shooting with a mechanical release aid. The release aid does not deflect the string as much as a release from the fingers. Hence, the arrow does not bend very much as it leaves the bow. Rather than the nock end of the arrow bending to the side of the arrow rest, the arrow is on a straighter course, and the fletching passes between the rest support arm and the handle. Shoot-through rests can be used with or without a cushion plunger [see (b) and (c), respectively, in Figure 18.6]. Adjustment of these arrow rests is also addressed in Step 16.

UPGRADING YOUR BOWSIGHT

You will particularly appreciate a tournament-quality bowsight if you have used a home-made sight. The advantage of a quality sight lies in the ease and precision of adjustment. This sight holds its setting without vibrating loose and remains true even when removed from the bow and replaced (see Figures 18.4 and 18.7).

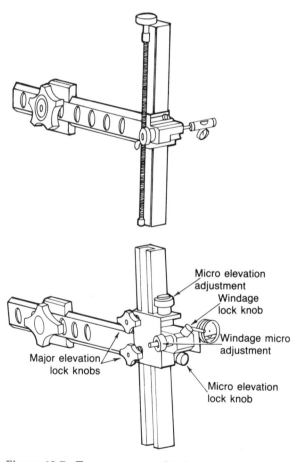

Figure 18.7 Tournament-quality bowsights.

You have a wide choice of apertures that can be installed in a quality sight (see Figure 18.8). A sight often has a level incorporated into the aperture so that you can always guard against canting the bow. Some rules, however, do not allow the use of levels. The aiming aperture used is largely a matter of personal preference; dots, crosshairs, posts, and open rings are the most popular. Some archers even use apertures with a light for an aiming dot because it can be seen more easily in dimly lit settings. Sight lenses that magnify the target are popular in competition equipment classifications that allow ''scopes.''

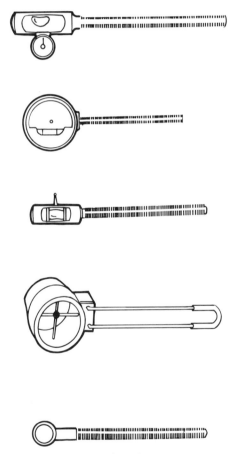

Figure 18.8 A variety of aiming apertures.

Where to mount the sight in relation to the bow is also a matter of preference. If you're like most archers, you'll prefer to position your sight on the back side of your bow and extended away from it. This allows finer sighting and makes an aiming dot relatively smaller in relation to the bull's-eye's center. An extended sight also magnifies movement of the bow arm in your perspective, so you need to experiment to find the position that gives you the finest aiming with a tolerable perception of movement. If you have a light-poundage bow, you may need to mount your sight on the face of the bow when shooting long distances. Otherwise, if you have mounted your sight on the back side of the bow, the aiming aperture may have to be positioned so low that it would interfere with the arrow in flight.

OTHER ACCESSORIES

Consider investing in the following additional accessories in order to increase your performance consistency.

Draw Checks

A draw check is an accessory that perhaps can be helpful to you. Even with a solid anchor position, there may be slight differences in the precise length of the draw from shot to shot. A draw check eliminates any variation.

Although there are several types of draw checks, the most common one is a clicker. There is a clicker mounted on the bow pictured in Figure 18.4. It is a single, flat piece of metal under which the arrow is placed when it is nocked. The arrow slides underneath it during the draw. The position of the clicker and length of the arrow are adjusted so that the clicker sits on the taper of the arrow tip when you reach full draw. You ready your shot, aim, then increase your back tension just enough so that the arrow tip slides from underneath the clicker. The clicker then strikes the bow, and you release upon hearing this sound. Hence, release occurs at exactly the same draw length on every shot.

Many archers use a clicker for reasons other than a check on draw length. For example, some find that they tend to release immediately when their sight is aligned with the bull's-eye without allowing the sight to settle. Attempts to overcome this tendency with practice fail, so they use a clicker as a means to release on an auditory signal, rather than on a visual one. Other archers have difficulty maintaining back tension throughout their shot, tending to collapse upon release. A clicker forces them to increase their back tension gradually until release.

Another type of draw check sometimes used by compound bow archers are cable stoppers. Two blocks are clamped onto the bow's cables. As the bow is drawn and the cables move, the two blocks approach each other until they are flush against each other at full draw. The string can be moved no farther back, so the draw length is identical from shot to shot. The blocks are set in position on the cables by trial and error to meet when the archer is at full draw.

Finger Tabs

You can experiment with a different type of finger tab if you have been using a simple piece of leather. Some tabs have several layers of materials, including felt and rubber in addition to leather. The layer that contacts the bowstring can be a smooth leather or animal hair. Some styles also have a piece of leather or felt beween the arrow nock and the fingers of your draw hand. This protects your fingers from rubbing on the nock and aids in a smooth release. An alternative is to have a thicker piece of plastic attached to the tab that lies between your first and middle fingers, preventing your fingers from squeezing the nock. It is also possible to buy a tab with an attached piece of plastic that touches your chin for a consistent anchor from shot to shot.

No matter what style of finger tab you prefer, be sure to use the correct size. It should be large enough to protect your fingers without being so large that it catches on the bowstring when released. A tab too large can be trimmed back for a better fit. Some archers sprinkle talcum powder on their tab for the smoothest release possible.

Spotting Aids

Competitive archers often buy a pair of binoculars or a spotting scope so they can check on the location of their arrows in the target. They can then adjust their sight during an end, rather than waiting until the end is completed and they approach the target to score. Small, light binoculars are popular indoors and in field archery, whereas spotting scopes placed on a tripod are popular for outdoor target shoots of long distance.

Bow Cases

Having upgraded your equipment and added accessories to your tackle, you ought to invest in an equipment or bow case to protect your tackle and transport it easily. Hard-sided cases are made for take-down recurves and compound bows. These cases also carry arrows, sights, and other accessories. Soft-sided cases are available for both recurve and compound bows and are less expensive, but they would make you carry most of your accessories separately.

USING A RELEASE AID

Shooting with a release aid is a popular form of archery for hunters and target archers alike. Because its use is not allowed by the governing bodies for amateur competition with recurve bows, most archers use the release aid only with compound bows. When used properly, the release aid allows more accurate shooting than possible with the fingers.

A single loop of rope or a small metal rod holds the string just below the arrow nock (see Figure 18.9). When you trigger the device, the release is cleaner than three, or even two, fingers coming off the string. The string deflection, pictured in Figure 18.1 with a finger release, is minimized with a release aid, so the arrow takes a straighter path to the target.

Release aids are available that are triggered with your index finger, thumb, or little finger. You must experiment to find the type that personally works best. Some archers believe the models that have you press a trigger rearward are superior to those in which you would trigger toward the target. Release aid or not, back tension is still a critical ingredient in shooting; pushing forward on a trigger can result in a slight loss of back tension. Some models also strap around the wrist, allowing you to draw with your back muscles while your hand is totally relaxed.

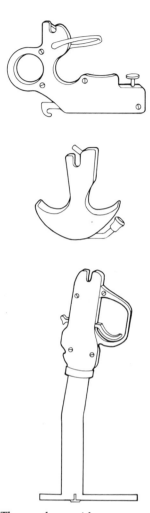

Figure 18.9   Three release aids.

The release aid must be triggered slowly so that the actual moment of release is almost a surprise to you. The most common fault in shooting a release aid is to anticipate or "punch" the release, which is similar to collapsing with a finger release because draw tension is reduced just at or slightly before release of the string.

Release aid shooters adapt their shooting form and equipment slightly from that common for finger shooters. Depending on the exact type of release aid, you anchor with the space between your first two base knuckles directly behind your jawbone. Your draw elbow may look higher and more directly in line to the target than that of the typical finger shooter. Because the release is so clean, you would probably use small vanes on your arrows. Your bow is set as close to center shot

as possible or exactly on center shot, and you use a shoot-through rest.

Release aid shooters are the most likely archers to use an overdraw. This is a device that extends the arrow rest toward you to permit use of a shorter—hence, lighter and faster—arrow (see Figure 18.10). Care must be taken with an overdraw because the arrow point is drawn behind your bow hand and could injure you if it slips off the rest at release. Overdraws that extend behind your bow wrist are also very critical because they tend to compound the effect of bow hand and wrist movement upon release. Therefore, the overdraw is best used by experienced archers. However, some manufacturers incorporate the benefits of the overdraw into their handle riser design by moving the grip back in relation to the limb attachment location.

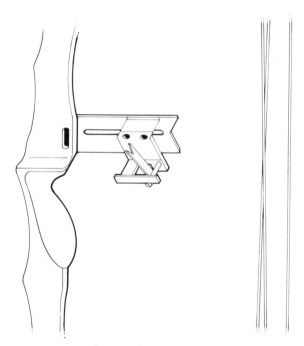

Figure 18.10   An overdraw.

UPGRADING YOUR EQUIPMENT FOR HUNTING

Hunting requires a different equipment setup than target archery, although many bowhunters join target competitions in equipment classifications in which only bowhunting equipment is allowed. The most popular type of bow for hunting is the compound bow. It

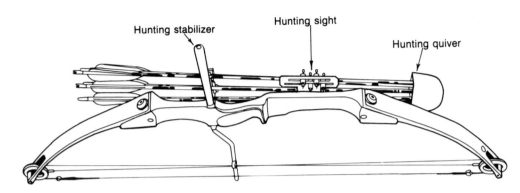

Figure 18.11   A compound bow typically used for hunting.

is shorter and easier to carry through the woods or shoot from a tree stand. The typical archer can shoot higher poundage with a compound bow, and this makes shooting more accurate. The archer typically estimates the distance from game. If a hunter's judgment is slightly in error, the flatter trajectory of an arrow shot from a heavier bow can still make it possible to kill the game. Deeper penetration into game is desirable because it maximizes the chances of killing, rather than just wounding, game, and recovering the game.

A compound bow set up for hunting is shown in Figure 18.11. Notice that the stabilizer is short so that it does not tangle in tree branches. For the same reason, the bowsight is not extended very far from the bow. The sight aperture is the pin style; there are 4 to 5 pins, each set for a different distance. Rather than having to adjust the pins before a shot, the hunter uses the pin preset for the distance at which the game is standing.

A hunting quiver is mounted on the side of the bow to keep arrows handy but the tackle compact. The hunting quiver has a hood to shield the broadheads mounted on the arrow tips. Broadheads come in a variety of styles, with two to six blades (see Figure 18.12a). Some are better suited to certain game, but there is a large degree of personal preference in the choice of broadheads. One thing all broadheads have in common is their sharpness. They must be handled with extreme care in order not to cut either the archer or the bowstring!

Bowhunters usually practice with field points installed on their arrows (see Figure

18.12b). They are closer in weight to broadheads than are target points. They can be easily replaced by a broadhead when hunting because both screw into the same insert. It is still necessary for hunters to "sight in" their broadheads. A large piece of Styrofoam is good for this purpose because broadheads ruin target butts quickly and are banned on most ranges.

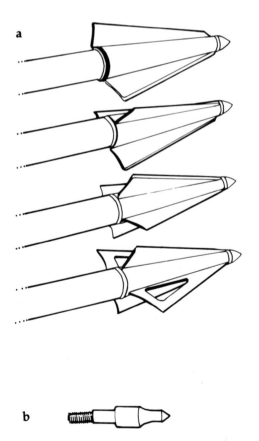

Figure 18.12   (a) Broadhead arrows used for hunting. (b) A screw-in field point.

Bowhunting equipment often comes in a dark color. Many archers then have a camouflage pattern painted onto the bows and accessories. Camouflaged clothing is worn from head to toe.

Bowhunting equipment must be durable because it is handled in wooded areas and subjected to extremes of temperature and moisture. A heavier arrow rest, less flexible but more durable than those for target shooting, can be installed. The bowhunters may sacrifice the cleaner release afforded by a finger tab for a shooting glove that attaches to the wrist and cannot be misplaced. Hunting arrow shafts are usually larger and heavier than a shaft the same archer uses for target shooting. This is necessitated in part by the heavy draw weight of the bow and in part by the weight of the broadhead. Larger fletching, most often of vanes, provides more stability in flight than small fletching, necessitated by the heavier arrow weight.

The bowhunter can use a range finder to more accurately judge the distance from game. From a fixed hunting location such as a tree stand, the distance to various landmarks is instantaneously given by the range finder. The bowhunter checks these distances when first arriving at the hunting location. Game walking up to these landmarks are then a known distance away.

UPGRADING YOUR EQUIPMENT FOR BOWFISHING

A bow adequate for bowfishing is not too different than the basic hunting bow, except that a reel is mounted on the bow at the base of the handle riser. This can be a drum reel or a heavy-duty spin fishing reel with the stabilizer incorporated (see Figure 18.13). The reel holds 50-90 feet of heavy line, which is attached to a solid fiberglass arrow.

The solid fiberglass arrow penetrates the water well. Most fishing arrows have rubber, slip-on fletching. The line is run through a hole near the nock, then a second hole through the arrow point and head of the shaft, where it is secured. Usually a barbed fish point is used so that fish cannot pull free.

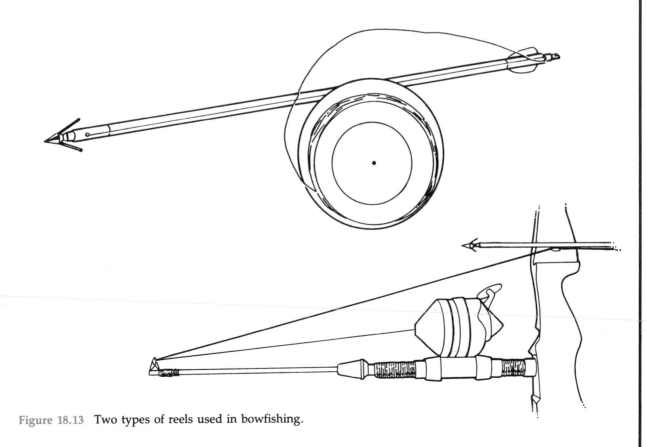

Figure 18.13 Two types of reels used in bowfishing.

Rating Your Total Progress

Each exercise you completed in this book had a success goal, which prompted your development of physical and mental skills. The following inventory allows you to rate your overall progress. Read the items carefully and respond to them thoughtfully.

PHYSICAL SKILLS

The first general success goal is acquiring the physical skills to shoot. How would you rate yourself on these aspects of your shooting?

Technique	Very Good	Good	Okay	Poor
Stance	_____	_____	_____	_____
Alignment	_____	_____	_____	_____
Anchor	_____	_____	_____	_____
Bow hand	_____	_____	_____	_____
Aiming	_____	_____	_____	_____
Release	_____	_____	_____	_____
Follow-through	_____	_____	_____	_____

Sighting				
Adjusting for windage	_____	_____	_____	_____
Adjusting for elevation	_____	_____	_____	_____
Adjusting for various distances	_____	_____	_____	_____
Shooting accuracy at short distances	_____	_____	_____	_____
Shooting accuracy at long distances	_____	_____	_____	_____
Adjusting and using accessories	_____	_____	_____	_____
Detecting your errors	_____	_____	_____	_____
Correcting your errors	_____	_____	_____	_____
Tournament procedures	_____	_____	_____	_____
Equipment maintenance	_____	_____	_____	_____
Equipment tuning	_____	_____	_____	_____

MENTAL SKILLS

The second general success goal is utilizing mental skills to improve performance. This is an area frequently overlooked, yet it has the potential to contribute measurably to shooting performance. How would you rate your ability to utilize these mental skills to your advantage?

	Very Good	Good	Okay	Poor
Concentration on aiming	_____	_____	_____	_____
Relaxation during the shot	_____	_____	_____	_____
Confidence in your next shot	_____	_____	_____	_____
Imagery	_____	_____	_____	_____

OVERALL ARCHERY PROGRESS

Considering all of the physical and mental factors you rated above, how would you rate your archery progress?

_____ Very successful

_____ Successful

_____ Barely successful

_____ Unsuccessful

Are you pleased with your progress?

_____ Very pleased

_____ Pleased

_____ Not pleased

Individual Program

INDIVIDUAL COURSE IN _____ GRADE/COURSE SECTION _____

STUDENT'S NAME _____ STUDENT ID # _____

SKILLS/CONCEPTS	TECHNIQUE AND PERFORMANCE OBJECTIVES	WT* ×	POINT PROGRESS** =				FINAL SCORE***
			1	2	3	4	

Note. From "The Role of Expert Knowledge Structures in an Instructional Design Model for Physical Education" by J.N. Vickers, 1983, *Journal of Teaching in Physical Education*, **2**(3), p. 17. Copyright 1983 by Joan N. Vickers. Adapted by permission.

*WT = Weighting of an objective's degree of difficulty.

**PROGRESS = Ongoing success, which may be expressed in terms of (a) accumulated points (1, 2, 3, 4); (b) grades (D, C, B, A); (c) symbols (merit, bronze, silver, gold); (d) unsatisfactory/satisfactory; and others as desired.

***FINAL SCORE equals WT times PROGRESS.

actual draw length The arrow length needed by an archer, measured from the bottom of the slit in the arrow nock to the back of the bow.

actual draw weight The energy required to draw the bow to the actual draw length, in pounds.

address To assume a stand straddling the shooting line.

aim To visually place a bowsight aperture over the target center; if a bowsight is not used, to visually place the arrow tip over a particular point.

afterhold The position of the body, head, and limbs after the string is released.

alignment With regard to the bowstring, the relationship between the string and sight aperture; with regard to shooting form, the relationship of the trunk and the arms.

anchor point A fixed position against the body to which the draw hand is brought, string in hand.

archer's paradox The manner in which the arrow clears the bow upon release by bending around the bow handle.

arm guard A piece of leather or plastic placed on the inside forearm of the bow arm to protect it from a slap of the bowstring upon release.

arrow plate A piece of plastic or leather glued to the bow window above the arrow rest.

arrow rest A projection from the bow window, above the arrow shelf, upon which the arrow lies when drawn.

arrow shelf A horizontal projection at the bottom of the bow window upon which the arrow can lie in the absence of an arrow rest.

arrow straightener A mechanical device used to detect and eliminate bends in aluminum arrows.

back The side of the bow limbs away from the archer at full draw.

bare shaft An arrow shaft without fletching of any kind.

barebow Shooting with no form of bowsight or aiming aid.

belly The side of the bow facing the archer at full draw; face.

Berger button A cushion plunger; a spring-loaded button mounted horizontally through the bow above the handle pivot point to absorb force as the arrow pushes against it upon release.

bolt The arrow shot by a crossbow.

bounce out An arrow that strikes the scoring area of the target face but rebounds away.

bow arm The arm of the hand that holds the bow.

bow bracer A device used to brace, or string, a bow.

bowfishing The sport of fishing with a bow.

bow hand The hand that holds the bow.

bowhunting The sport of hunting with a bow.

bow scale A mechanical device that measures the draw weight of a bow at any stage of the draw.

bowsight Any device mounted on the bow that allows an archer to aim directly at the target or a mark.

bow sling A strap attached to the bow through which the archer slips the bow hand, thereby preventing the bow from being dropped upon release.

bow square A device that attaches to the bowstring and lies on the arrow rest to measure brace height and nocking point location.

bowstring The string on the bow, usually made of Dacron or Kevlar.

bow stringer A device used to brace, or string, a bow.

bow window The recessed area above the grip; sight window.

bowyer A maker of bows.

brace To place the string on the bow.

brace height The distance between the bow, measured at the pivot point, and string when the bow is strung; string height.

broadhead A multiply edged sharp arrow point used in hunting game.

bull's-eye   The area on the target face with the highest scoring value, usually in the center.

butt   A backstop for arrows made of grasses, excelsior, straw, cardboard, polyethylene foam or fiber.

cam bow   A type of compound bow with oval-shaped eccentric pulleys.

cant   To tilt the bow to the right or left, as indicated by the top limb tip, at full draw.

cast   The ability of a bow to project an arrow; the distance and speed a bow can shoot an arrow.

center serving   The wrapping thread over the center of the bowstring, where the arrow is nocked.

chest protector   A piece of nylon netting or vinyl worn over the clothing to prevent the bowstring from catching.

clicker   A device attached to the bow or sometimes on a compound bow to the cables that indicates by sound that the arrow has been drawn to a certain desired distance; most archers use its click as an indication to release.

closed stance   A shooting stance in which an imaginary straight line to the target intersects the toes of the rear foot and middle of the front foot.

clout   An archery game of long-distance shooting at a 48-foot target laid out flat on the ground.

cock feather   The feather mounted at a right angle to the nock, often of a distinct color; index feather.

collapse   A form error in which the archer eases up, losing muscle control, at release.

Columbia round   A competitive round shot from 50, 40, and 30 yards at a 48-inch target face; 24 arrows are shot at each distance.

composite bow   A bow made of two or more different materials.

compound bow   A bow using a cable system attached to eccentric pulleys mounted at the limb tips, producing peak resistance at mid-draw, then dropping off to hold weight less than the draw weight.

creeping   Allowing the draw hand to move forward immediately before or during release.

crest   Markings on the arrow shaft, usually colored bands near the fletching.

crosshair sight   A sight with a circular aperture in which two fine lines cross at right angles; the intersection of the lines is aimed at the target.

cushion plunger   A spring-loaded button mounted horizontally through the bow above the handle pivot point to absorb force as the arrow pushes against it upon release.

dead release   A bowstring release wherein the archer opens the string fingers but the hand moves little if at all.

draw   Pulling the bowstring.

draw check   A device attached to the bow to indicate that full draw has been reached.

draw hand   The hand that holds the bowstring.

draw fingers   The fingers used to draw the bowstring.

draw length   The distance between the nocking point and the grip of the bow at full draw; at one time, draw length was measured to the back of the bow.

draw weight   The number of pounds required to draw any bow a given distance.

drift   Lateral displacement, due to crosswind, of an arrow flying toward the target.

dynabow   A compound bow with a cam on one bow tip but no eccentric pulley on the other.

eccentric pulley   A round wheel mounted at the limb tip, used to decrease the amount of weight held on the bowstring at full draw.

end   A specified number of arrows shot before archers go to the target to score and retrieve their arrows.

face   The side of the bow facing the archer at full draw; the belly of the bow. Also, the paper or cardboard with a target printed on it.

field archery   A type of competitive archery shot outdoors in a wooded area, with targets of varying distances and sizes; archers walk from target to target.

field captain   The official in charge of the archery range during a tournament, traditionally a male official.

field point   An arrow point that is heavier than a target point and similar in weight to a broadhead; it can be unscrewed from a mounting insert in aluminum arrows so a broadhead can be installed.

finger sling A piece of leather, plastic, or rope looped at each end through which the archer slips the thumb and a finger after taking hold of the bow, permitting a loose grip.

finger tab A piece of leather or plastic worn over the draw fingers both to protect them and to ensure a smooth release of the bowstring.

fishtailing A back-and-forth motion of the nock end of an arrow on its flight to the target.

fistmele Brace height.

FITA Federation Internationale de Tir a L'Arc, the International Target Archery Federation, which conducts world championship archery contests for the recurve bow. Also, the championship round used in such contests.

fletching The turkey feathers or plastic vanes mounted on an arrow to stabilize it in flight.

fletching jig The device used to hold a feather or vane in place against the arrow shaft as the fletching cement dries.

flight shooting A form of archery in which the object is to shoot an arrow for the greatest distance possible.

flinching A form error in which the bow arm moves suddenly upon release, usually flexing horizontally at the bow shoulder.

flu-flu An arrow with large fletching mounted in a continuous spiral, sometimes used for wing shooting because the fletching slows the arrow after an initial flight stage of normal velocity.

follow-through The archer's position after release of the arrow; ideally, the body, head, and bow arm position are held steady, and the draw hand recoils over the draw shoulder as a result of continuous back tension.

foot marker Anything used to mark the exact position of the feet in addressing the target, so that the archer can duplicate the position and distance from the target on subsequent shots.

force-draw curve The graph created by plotting draw weight (vertical axis) against draw length (horizontal axis) for a bow as it is drawn to full draw.

freestyle An equipment classification that typically allows free use of mechanical devices to improve accuracy.

freeze A shooting flaw wherein the archer aims outside the bull's-eye and cannot move the sight aperture into the center. Also, inability to release an arrow.

full draw The position wherein the bowstring is moved back and the draw hand anchors with respect to the head and neck.

gap shooting Aiming by associating the space seen between the arrow tip and the target with the shooting distance.

glove A leather covering that slips over the draw finger tips and attaches to the wrist to protect the draw fingers and allow a smooth release; an alternative to a finger tab.

gold The center area of the multicolored target often used in target archery.

gold fever An inability to hold the bowsight in the bull's-eye.

grip The part of the bow handle where the bow is held. Also, the removable plastic piece that allows a change in the shape of the bow where it is held.

ground quiver An arrow holder that sits on or sticks into the ground; some also hold a bow.

grouping The pattern of an archer's arrows in the target.

handle The middle section of the bow.

handle riser The middle section of the bow exclusive of the limbs.

hanging arrow An arrow that penetrates the target face but not the butt and hangs across the target face.

heeling A shooting flaw in which the archer pushes forward suddenly with the heel of the bow hand.

hen feathers The two feathers at oblique angles to the nock slit, usually the same color as each other but of a different color than the index, or cock, feather.

high anchor An anchor position wherein the draw hand contacts the side of the face.

high wrist The bow hold position in which the top of the wrist is held level with the top of the bow arm.

hit   A shot that lands within the scoring area of a target face.

holding   Maintaining steady bow position at full draw during aiming.

index feather   The feather mounted on an arrow shaft at a right angle to the nock slit, often of a distinct color; the cock feather.

jerking   A shooting flaw in which the draw hand is pulled suddenly back or down as the bowstring is released.

jig   A device that holds feathers or vanes on an arrow shaft until the fletching cement dries. Also, a device with adjustable posts around which Dacron or Kevlar is wound to make a bowstring.

kisser button   A small disk attached to the bowstring meant to contact the lips in the anchor position to assure proper anchor and head positions.

Lady Paramount   The official, traditionally a woman, in charge of an archery tournament.

laminated bow   A bow made by bonding together a number of pieces of material to take advantage of the good qualities of each.

let down   A return to the ready position without releasing the bowstring.

let-off   The weight reduction from peak weight to holding weight on a compound bow.

level   A device attached to the sight or the bow to help the archer maintain a vertical bow position.

limbs   The energy-storing parts of a bow above and below the handle riser section.

longbow   A bow style popular in England in the Middle Ages; long limbs without a recurve shape are characteristic of long bows. Although not as efficient in design as a bow with recurved limbs, the longbow does not require the bonding together of materials, especially difficult in the past in the damp weather of England.

loop   The served bend at the end of a bowstring; it fits into the limb notches of a recurve bow or the teardrop at the end of the cable of a compound bow.

loose   A dated term meaning to release the bowstring.

low wrist   A bow hand position wherein the hand is flat against the bow handle and the pressure during draw is through the forearm bone.

mass weight   The physical weight of the bow and the attached accessories.

mat   A target butt, usually made of tightly packed grasses and circular in shape.

misnocking   The arrow falling from the bow at release instead of flying toward the target, resulting from the bowstring not being in contact with the arrow nock.

NAA   The National Archery Association, the United States organization that oversees competition with the recurve bow for amateur archers.

NFAA   The National Field Archery Association, the United States organization that oversees field archery and indoor competition for various equipment classifications.

nock   The removable piece, usually plastic, on the end of an arrow, with a slit for the bowstring.

nocking   Placing the arrow on the bowstring in preparation for shooting.

nock locator   A stop on the bowstring against which the arrow is placed.

nocking point   The location on the bowstring where the nock locator is positioned.

notch   The groove at the end of the limb tip of a recurve bow into which the bowstring is seated.

oblique stance   Usually an open stance, but occasionally any stance other than a square stance.

open stance   A position on the shooting line wherein a straight line to the target passes through the middle of the rear foot and the toes of the front foot.

overbowed   Using a bow too heavy to allow the archer to shoot continuously with good form.

overdraw   To draw an arrow so that the point passes the face of the bow. Also, a device that permits use of arrows shorter than the archer's draw length.

overstrung   A condition in which a bow is strung with a bowstring too short, making the brace height too high.

PAA   The Professional Archer's Association, which oversees competition for professional archers.

pass through An arrow that penetrates completely through the target face and target butt.

peak weight The highest weight achieved during the draw of a compound bow.

peeking A shooting flaw wherein the archer moves the head at release in order to watch the arrow in flight.

peep sight A plastic or metal piece with a small hole, tied into the bowstring so that the archer can look through the hole to line up the bowsight and target.

perfect end An end in which all arrows land in the highest scoring area.

petticoat The perimeter of the target face, outside the scoring area.

pile The arrow point.

pin sight A sight using one or more sight apertures similar to a pin head.

pinching Squeezing the arrow nock with the draw fingers during the draw.

pivot point The place on the bow's grip that is farthest from the string.

plucking A shooting flaw in which the draw hand is pulled away from the face and body upon release.

point The arrow tip.

point-of-aim A method of aiming in which the arrow point is aligned with some point in front of and below the target.

post sight A bowsight with an aperture having a metal piece projecting vertically up or down, the tip of which is aligned with the bull's-eye.

powder pouch A container for talcum or similar powder, often used to dry an archer's hands or applied to the finger tab for a smoother release.

pressure point The place on the arrow plate against which the arrow pushes upon release of the bowstring.

pull To remove shot arrows from the target. Also, to draw the bow.

pushing Moving the bow forward and away from the archer during release and follow-through.

quiver A holder for arrows that may be worn, placed on the ground, or mounted on the bow, the latter particularly when hunting.

range The place where archery shooting takes place. Also, the distance to be shot.

rebound An arrow that hits the target face but bounces back toward the archer, rather than penetrating the target; a bounce-out.

recurved bow A bow with limb tips that are curved forward.

reflexed bow A bow that appears bent backward when unstrung; it does not necessarily have recurved limb tips, though.

release Letting go of the bowstring, ideally by relaxation of the draw finger hook.

release aid A hand-held device attached to the bowstring used to draw and release the string, minimizing the string deflection otherwise seen with release by the fingers.

ring sight A bowsight with an aperture that is an open circle; the bull's-eye is centered in the ring to aim the arrow.

riser The center, handle portion of the bow exclusive of the limbs.

round The number of ends shot at designated distances and target sizes to obtain a standard score.

roving An archery game in which a group of archers in the woods, one following another, shoot at random targets at unknown distances as designated by the first archer.

scatter The arrow grouping wherein shots are spread out over the target face or shooting area.

scoring area The part of the target face made up of scoring circles.

self A bow or arrow made from a single piece of wood.

serving A heavy thread wrapped around the bowstring at its center and on the loops to protect the string and to add strength.

shaft The body of an arrow.

shelf A horizontal projection at the bottom of the bow window, upon which the arrow can lie in the absence of an arrow rest.

shooting glove A leather covering that slips over the draw fingertips and attaches around the wrist, protecting the draw fingers and allowing a smooth release; an alternative to a finger tab.

shooting line A marked line parallel to the targets, from which all archers shoot.

sight Any device mounted on the bow that allows the archer to aim directly at the target or a mark.

sight bar The part of the bowsight to which the aperture assembly is attached.

sight extension A bar that allows the bowsight to be extended from the bow toward the target.

sight pin A bowsight aperture that is a straight piece of metal with a dot or ball at the end.

sight window The recessed area above the grip; bow window.

six golds A perfect end of six arrows.

skirt An outer cloth on some target faces that holds the face on the target mat; the petticoat.

sling A strap attached to the bow or to the hand holding the bow, thereby preventing the bow from dropping to the ground upon release.

snap shooting A shooting flaw wherein the arrow is shot immediately as the bowsight crosses the bull's-eye.

spine The measured deflection of an arrow shaft, established by hanging a 2-pound weight from its center.

spiral fletch A certain angled position of the fletching on an arrow shaft.

springy A small spring with an arrow rest extension substituted for a cushion plunger.

stabilizer A rod-and-weight assembly mounted on either the face or back of the handle riser to help eliminate torque of the bow around its long axis upon release.

stacking A rapid, disproportionate increase in draw weight in the last few inches of draw in some recurve bows.

stance The foot position taken to address the target.

string The bowstring. Also, to attach the bowstring to the limb tip by bending the bow limbs, placing them under tension.

string alignment The relationship between the bowstring and the sight aperture.

string fingers The fingers that hold the bowstring in shooting the bow.

string height The distance between the bow, measured at the pivot point, and the string when the bow is strung; brace height.

string notch The groove at the end of the limb tip of a recurve bow into which the bowstring is seated.

string pattern The relationship between the bowstring and the sight aperture.

string peep A plastic or metal piece with a small hole, tied into the bowstring above the nock locator so that the archer can look through the hole to line up the bowsight and target.

string walking A style of shooting wherein the archer moves the position of the draw fingers on the string to adjust the vertical displacement of the arrow; no bowsight is used.

tab A piece of leather or plastic worn over the draw fingers both to protect them and to ensure a smooth release of the bowstring; finger tab.

tackle The archer's equipment.

take-down bow A bow with detachable limbs.

target butt The backstop for arrows, made of grasses, excelsior, straw, cardboard, polyethylene foam or fiber.

target captain The person at each target during a tournament designated to call the scoring value of all arrows on that target.

target face The paper or cardboard scoring area mounted on the target butt.

target mat A butt of tightly packed grasses, usually circular in shape.

target panic The inability to hold the sight on the bull's-eye long enough to steady the bow before release.

tiller A measure of even balance in the two limbs; on a compound bow, tiller is adjustable through the limb bolts, thus varying the distance between the base of the limb and the string.

tip The end of a bow limb; arrow point.

torque A rotation of the bow about its long axis upon release of the bowstring.

toxophilite An archer.

trajectory The parabolic path of an arrow in flight.

tuning Adjustment of the arrow spine, arrow rest, pressure point, cushion plunger, string height, tiller, and nocking point to achieve the truest arrow flight possible.

underbowed Use of a bow too light in draw weight.

understrung A bow with a string too long, resulting in a low brace height and reduced efficiency.

valley The point of lowest holding weight reached near full draw on a compound bow.

vane A plastic fletching that is more wind- and weatherproof than feathers, but often heavier.

weight The number of pounds of force required to draw the bowstring a given distance.

windage Horizontal correction of the bowsight setting to compensate for drift due to wind.

wrist sling A strap that wraps around the archer's wrist and the bow, thereby preventing the bow from falling to the ground at release.

yaw An arrow's erratic motion during its flight to the target.

Kathleen M. Haywood, PhD, is associate professor of physical education at the University of Missouri–St. Louis and is a member of the Professional Archers Association and the professional division of the National Field Archery Association. On the professional tour she is sponsored by the Ludwikoski-Wortman distributors of Golden Eagle bows and is a member of the Saunders Archery Company product-testing team.

An eight-time Missouri state champion, in 1985 Dr. Haywood was both the indoor and outdoor Midwest Sectional champion of the National Field Archery Association. In addition to giving private instruction, she has taught archery at Washington University and the University of Illinois. Widely published in such journals as *Research Quarterly for Exercise and Sport*, the *British Journal of Sports Medicine*, the *Journal of Sport Sciences*, and the *Journal of Motor Behavior*, Dr. Haywood is also the author of *Life Span Motor Development* (Human Kinetics Publishers, 1986). Her recreational activities include jogging, softball, and tennis.

Catherine F. Lewis, MEd, teaches elementary physical education at the Andrews Academy in Creve Coeur, Missouri. In 1983 she was the Midwest Sectional indoor champion of the National Field Archery Association, belonging to that group's professional division as well as the Professional Archers Association. Ms. Lewis is an exceptional teacher, having taught archery in the professional preparation program at the University of Missouri–St. Louis and to youths in school, scouting, and camp programs. When not teaching or entered in archery competitions, she devotes her leisure time to softball, camping, and fishing.